MAXIE DUNNAM

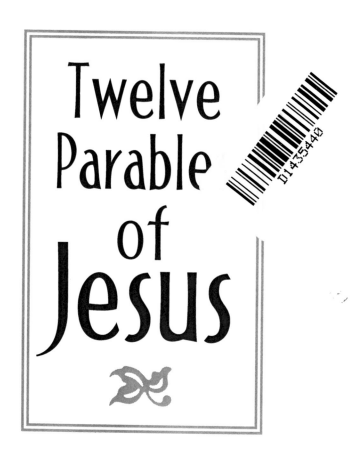

Twelve
Parable
of
Jesus

BIBLE STUDY FOR CHRISTIAN LIVING

Abingdon Press | Nashville

Twelve Parables of Jesus

Copyright © 1988 by Cokesbury
Abingdon Press edition published 2006

All rights reserved.

ISBN 0-687-49000-6

Scripture quotations unless otherwise marked are from the Revised Standard Version of the Bible, copyright © 1946, 1952, © 1971 by the Division of Christian Education of the National Council of the Churches of Christ in the United States of America. Used by permission. All rights reserved.

Information in the sections entitled "For further reflection" at the end of each chapter owes much to *The Parables of Jesus*, by Joachim Jeremias; Charles Scribner's Sons, © 1963 SCM Press Ltd.

Contents

"He Said Nothing to Them Without a Parable"

Introduction

Tell me a story, Daddy. That's a recurring request in families. Much of the life and history and tradition of families is passed on by stories. Much of the learning that takes place in people takes place through storytelling.

No tradition is richer with stories than the Jewish tradition of which Jesus was a part. And Jesus, following in that rabbinic line, was a master storyteller.

One of the master storytellers of our time is Elie Wiesel. In the introduction to his book, *Souls on Fire* (Summitt Books, 1982), he said, "My father, an enlightened spirit, believed in man. My grandfather, a fervent hassid, believed in God. The one taught me to speak, the other to sing. Both loved stories. And when I tell mine, I hear their voices. Whispering from beyond the silent story, they are what links the survivors to their memory."

There is a sense in which the stories that Jesus told are what links us to him. They paint word pictures that enter our thoughts and imaginations in a way we can't forget. More than any other source, they bring to life the world in which Jesus lived.

> We read the parables and the poor homes of that little land are before our eyes. We see the baking of bread and the patching of garments; we see even the emergency of a friend borrowing a loaf at midnight for his sudden guests. Rich homes are drawn with a pencil equally shrewd—barns bursting with fatness, laborers not daring to eat until

their master has broken his fast, and the unseemingly scramble for the chief seats at the feasts of the mighty. The glaring contrasts of our earth are drawn in dramatic line—"chosen" Jews and despised Samaritans, sumptuous Dives and abject Lazarus, householders and thieves, compassionate parenthood and the rascally steward who feathered his nest against the well-merited retribution. The whole gamut of human life is sounded—farmers at the plough, fishermen at their nets, a wedding procession moving through the dark with dancing torches, builders rearing towers, kings marching to their wars, and a widow pleading her cause in the persistence of despair before a heartless judge. (*The Parables of Jesus*, by George A. Buttrick (Baker, 1973); pages xviii–xix)

Through the parables we see the world in which Jesus lived. But more important, the parables can lead us into the mind and spirit of Jesus, into the way he was able to discern in the events of everyday life, lessons for living in the kingdom of God.

More than one-third of Jesus' recorded teaching is in the form of parables, the unique stories he told. Matthew, Mark, and John all report that in his teaching "he said nothing to them without a parable" (Matthew 13:34). Mark adds, "With many such parables he spoke the word to them, as they were able to hear it" (4:33).

Why did Jesus choose to teach in parables? A story catches the attention, fires the imagination, and allows the hearers to receive the message according to their ability to understand and accept it. A story disarms hostility. We find ourselves identifying with the characters in a parable and acknowledging its truth, when we might resist or reject an exhortation. Because we enter so fully into the parables, they inspire us to respond and to act.

Jesus' parables stand alone: They defy comparison. So, we will study some of those parables. We will not be able to consider them all, but in each chapter we will focus on one or two parables, let them link us with Jesus, and help us learn from him. We will try to get beyond the story to the message and behind the message to the Messenger—Jesus himself.

My prayer is that these familiar parables of our Lord may come alive anew in your life and that you may be blessed by their power to enlighten and to transform.

1. WHAT TO DO WHILE WAITING FOR THE JUDGMENT

Wise and Foolish Virgins

Read Matthew 25:1-13

Who hasn't had the experience of being unready for a long-awaited guest? A thousand things have hindered our preparation. An unexpected phone call kept us late at the office. Traffic on the freeway was tied up by an accident. The supermarket was crowded and we ended up in the slowest check-out line. The oven won't heat. The cat has walked down the middle of the table we set this morning leaving unmistakable, sooty footprints. And our six-year-old knocks over a cup of milk. Then time runs out. The guest is at the door. We have lost the opportunity for a leisurely visit; we must struggle instead with dinner preparations. For all of us, in large matters and small, a time of judgment inevitably comes. Time runs out. We have no more second chances.

In this chapter we're dealing with the parable of the wise and foolish virgins. Jesus was comparing the kingdom of heaven to a wedding feast. George Buttrick said of this parable:

> Jesus came to woo and win mankind to his own joy. Luke assigns the parable to the last week of His earthly life. That striking context is not disproved by the gladsomeness of the figure, for we have assurance elsewhere that the valedictory of Jesus to His disciples was the gift of gladness: "These things have I spoken unto you that My joy may be in you, and that your joy may be full." (*The Parables of Jesus* (Baker, 1973); page 234)

9

How especially tragic it is when our failure to be prepared shuts us out of life's most joyous invitation! This parable lays open the blatant excuses we human beings make for our actions and for our failure to act. We even make excuses in our relationship to God. But we can, in truth, play no such tricks. God knows us better than we know ourselves. There's no way to evade the consequences of our own acts and attitudes, and that's what this parable of Jesus is about. Therefore, our theme is "What to Do While Waiting for the Judgment."

Someone Is Coming

When Jesus described the kingdom of God or taught about judgment, he often used the image of someone or something coming and the need to be prepared. The Kingdom comes like a thief in the night, like a flood, like a master returning from a journey, or like a long-delayed bridegroom. The first chapter of John's Gospel records the world's unreadiness for Jesus' own coming: "He was in the world, and the world was made through him, yet the world knew him not. He came to his own home, and his own people received him not" (John 1:10-11). What a tragic loss for those who were not prepared to receive Jesus! For "to all who received him, who believed in his name, he gave power to become children of God" (verse 12).

Jesus begins his parable of the wise and foolish virgins with the words, "The kingdom of heaven shall be compared to ten maidens who took their lamps and went to meet the bridegroom." Undoubtedly, Christians in the early church identified Jesus as the bridegroom. They expected Jesus would return very soon bringing the kingdom of heaven on earth. Perhaps when Jesus did not return as they had expected, this parable helped them accept and better understand Jesus' words, "For the Son of man is coming at an hour you do not expect." But what about us? For whose coming do we prepare? How do we understand the kingdom of heaven?

Do we interpret this parable as a command to be ready for Christ's return whenever that event takes place? The answer is a resounding *yes.* Do we interpret it as teaching us to be ready for our own deaths and for life after death? Yes, of course. But Jesus is also calling us to be spiritually prepared for the kingdom of heaven that is in our midst. In other places, Jesus tells his disciples to watch and pray that they may not yield to temptation. He speaks of the need to be prepared for sorrow, for persecution, for calamity. But here Jesus is saying, "Be prepared for joy. Be ready for the wedding feast."

10

In his book, *Telling the Truth: The Gospel as Tragedy, Comedy, and Fairy Tale*, Frederick Buechner says,

> People are prepared for everything except for the fact that beyond the darkness of their blindness there is a great light. They are prepared to go on breaking their backs plowing the same old field until the cows come home without seeing, until they stub their toes on it, that there is a treasure buried in that field rich enough to buy Texas. They are prepared for a God who strikes hard bargains but not for a God who gives as much for an hour's work as for a day's. They are prepared for a mustard-seed kingdom of God no bigger than the eye of a newt but not for the great banyan it becomes with birds in its branches singing Mozart. They are prepared for the potluck supper at First Presbyterian but not for the marriage supper of the lamb, and when the bridegroom finally arrives at midnight with vineleaves in his hair, they turn up with their lamps to light him on his way all right only they have forgotten the oil to light them with. . . . ((Harper & Row, 1977); page 70)

That is true of us, isn't it? Our most bitter regrets come, not because we were not prepared for the worst, but because we were not prepared for the best. How often we miss golden opportunities because we are not prepared for them! The same is true of nations. How much more readily we prepare for war than for peace. How quick we are to meet the needs of disaster victims, but how slow to plan the use of our resources in such a way that famine, flood, and pollution will no longer plague humanity. The moment of judgment comes on our failure to prepare for the best no less than upon our failure to be ready for the worst. The foolish maidens were not prepared for the bridegroom's delay. They had no reserves of oil for their lamps so they were shut out of the long-anticipated marriage feast.

The Door Was Shut

In this parable of the wise and foolish virgins, the moment of judgment is expressed in the words, "The door was shut." I believe the primary teaching of the parable is caught in those resounding words, "the door was shut."

Do you hear the finality in that phrase? The door was shut. Boom—the door was shut!

Have you ever been to a theater production where the doors were closed as the performance began? If you got there one minute after the doors were shut, they wouldn't let you in until the intermission. How angry you became, or if not angry, how disappointed. But you could rest in the fact that thirty or forty minutes later at intermission time, you could get in.

But there's no intermission time suggested here. It's final. The door was shut.

What a graphic metaphor for judgment! Now I don't know where you are in your thinking about judgment—especially about a "Day of Judgment." A lot of Christians have gotten away from notions like that. But there is no way you can edit out the notion of judgment, either in the Bible or in life itself. You may naively think you can. You may sneer at radio and television preachers who do nothing but preach about the Last Judgment and preach about it as though they're gloating in the fact that they're going to get to heaven and you're going to be left out. But don't let the overemphasis on judgment in some quarters blind you to the fact that Scripture witnesses that both persons and nations stand in judgment before God. God's judgment is an essential part of the biblical understanding of life. God created the world, called it good, and set before human beings the choice of good and evil. Life depends upon that choice.

Scripture makes clear God's judgment on injustice and unrighteousness. The door was shut! Adam and Eve were cast out of the Garden of Eden because of their disobedience. Cain was made a wanderer on the face of the earth because he murdered his brother. God sent Moses to deliver the Hebrews from slavery and persecution in Egypt, to demand of Pharaoh, "Let my people go." Amos spoke of the Day of the Lord that would bring, not victory, but punishment of Israel's sins. The prophet, Malachi, described vividly what he thought the Day of Judgment would be like. After listing Israel's many sins, he says, "For behold, the day comes, burning like an oven, when all the arrogant and all evildoers will be stubble; the day that comes shall burn them up, says the Lord of hosts, so that it will leave them neither root nor branch" (Malachi 4:1).

Book after book in the Bible . . . sound a similar note: There will be a Day of Judgment—a day of darkness, a day of chaos, a day of fear and

12

flight, a day of starvation and agony, a day of fire. So characteristic is this emphasis that we're forced in all honesty to say that the somber note of judgment—the judgment of God—is an essential part of the Bible and biblical thought on life and history. (*He Spoke to Them in Parables*, by Harold A. Bosley (Harper & Row, 1963); page 46)

And don't think judgment is restricted to the Old Testament. It's not surprising that this parable of the wise and foolish virgins is recorded by Matthew. There is a sense in which the Gospel of Matthew might be called "The Gospel of Judgment." More than all the other Gospels, it deals with the notion of divine judgment in history and a Day of Judgment at the end of history. Matthew devotes two full chapters—Chapters 24 and 25—to Jesus' words about divine judgment and to his stern warning to the disciples to be ready for the day of tribulation, for the day of reckoning when the master returns, for the appearance of the Son of man.

Chapter 24 includes Jesus' foretelling the destruction of the Temple because of the disobedience of Israel. Then Jesus gives a vivid picture of the days immediately before the Day of Judgment when the Son of man will come with his angels to judge the world. He warns his disciples, "Therefore you also must be ready; for the Son of man is coming at an hour you do not expect." The chapter concludes with a parable about the reward of servants who are faithful when their master is away and the punishment of servants who are unfaithful.

Chapter 25 includes three very familiar parables about judgment and about being prepared at all times. In the parable we're considering here, Jesus tells of the wise and foolish virgins, some of whom were ready for their Lord's coming. But some were not ready, and for them the door would be shut and they would be utterly rejected. In the parable of the talents, which we will study in Chapter 11, Jesus urges his hearers to invest all they have in time and money for his sake—against his sudden appearing.

Then comes the most famous parable of judgment. The Son of man, surrounded by his angels, sits on his glorious throne and nations of people pass in review. He separates them into groups: one to be rewarded and one to be punished. This parable is so well known we hardly need to repeat the why of judgment—"Inasmuch as you did it unto one of the least of these my brethren, you did it unto me" or "Inasmuch as you did it not unto one of the least of these my brethren, you did it not unto me."

Jesus is clear in his teaching. God is good and demands of us a life of right-eousness. God is not neutral; sin is serious to God. He expects obedience in the ordinary, day-to-day relationships of life. He lays down his demands of us to go beyond self and self-service and to meet the needs of others.

The bottom line of it all is this: The time comes when all our second chances have run out. Let that truth burn in our minds. Do you hear that ringing word? The door was shut!

However, I would never call persons to live in fear—we don't need to live in fear. I would never seek to exercise that preacher ploy of picturing God as an angry judge holding persons by a spider web over a raging pit of fire. But I would want you to keep that word from the parable echoing in your heart: The door was shut! The time comes when all our second chances have run out.

Ready or Not

Now with that notion of judgment firmly in our minds—let's relate ourselves to it by looking at the wise and the foolish virgins. They are alike outwardly. Alike in knowledge and ignorance, alike in intention, alike in human frailty—they all fell asleep while waiting for the bridegroom to appear. But there was a life-and-death difference: Preparedness.

I titled this chapter, "What To Do While Waiting for the Judgment." The way to be ready for tomorrow is to be ready for today. The reason the foolish virgins didn't get into the wedding feast was that they had no oil. All the years that I've read this parable, I had not gotten that point until I was preparing this chapter. I thought these five foolish virgins were simply so late when they returned from getting oil. But the Scripture doesn't say that. There's not anything about their having oil when they returned, only that they wanted to get in. I believe it is true to the mind and character of Christ that if they had found oil, they would have gotten in.

To the persons who are ready, the door is always open. They are ready come what may. So, thus the truth: *The best way to get ready for tomorrow is to be ready for today.*

The great Quaker thinker and writer, Thomas R. Kelly, recognized this truth. On a trip to Europe at the beginning of the second World War he observed, "The last vestige of earthly security is gone. *It has always been gone*, and religion has always said so, but we haven't believed it." In a call for "Holy Obedience" he wrote:

> One returns from Europe with the sound of weeping in one's ears in order to say, "Don't be deceived. *You* must face Destiny. Preparation is only possible now. Don't be fooled by your sunny skies. When the rains descend and the floods come and the winds blow and beat upon *your* house, your private dwelling, your own family, your own fair hopes, your own strong muscles, your own body, your own soul itself, then it is well-nigh too late to build a house. You can only go inside what house you have and pray that it is founded upon the Rock." (*A Testament of Devotion* (Harper Row, 1941); page 69)

A time comes when no further preparation is possible, but if we have prepared for today, we will be ready for every tomorrow.

Substituting Form for Substance

Before we look further at ways we prepare for today and tomorrow, I want us to look at a suggestion in the parable that is not central to it, but that certainly is worthy of note. Jesus taught this idea elsewhere; therefore, I don't want to pass it by.

The truth is this: We tend to substitute form for function, organization for ministry, machinery for power, the instrument for its purpose. In other words, like the virgins whom we have come to call foolish, we possess lamps all right, but we lack the oil to make them burn.

We can talk about that in terms of our national life—our government. Don't you think political candidates' lack of real substance is the reason that not many people get super excited about elections?

Look at labor and industry in our nation. We have the genius and the productive powers unequaled in the history of civilization—yet our whole industrial and productive system is in trouble. Not only are we in trouble in this nation because our industry is not competitive with systems around the world, there is a graver problem that is a moral issue.

In a world that desperately needs a lifting of its material standards of living, we ought to have a field day. Strangely enough, we stumble and often miss our opportunities and bungle our chances. The lamps are there but they cast a dim, uncertain, and smoking light. They seem to be going out, and the cry at midnight too often finds us out of fuel. (*The Parables*, by Gerald Kennedy (Harper & Brothers, 1960); page 125)

Something is wrong, at the heart of things, in a nation such as ours when we create a welfare system that keeps people forever in a cycle of bondage to poverty. We could find the creative genius and the wherewithal to change the system if we had fuel for our lamps.

Marriage and family is certainly one of those institutions that seems to be running out of fuel. Nearly half of the marriages in our country each year still end in divorce. Many that are not ending in divorce are ravaged with selfishness and deceit and unfaithfulness. Children have a surfeit of toys but a deficiency of love. Parents invest themselves in their own selfish pursuits far more than they do in each other and in their children. The power that makes marriage creative and enduring is missing. That power is centered in love that is possible only through a relationship with God and Jesus Christ and through a commitment for better or worse, for richer or poorer, in sickness and in health. The kind of love that Paul described is a love that is patient and kind—not jealous or boastful, not arrogant or rude. A love that does not insist on its own way—is not irritable or resentful, that does not rejoice in the wrong, but rejoices in the right. A love that bears all things, believes all things, hopes all things, endures all things (1 Corinthians 13:4-7).

We have forgotten, or we never learned, that it takes three to get married: a man and a woman and God!

The church hasn't escaped the dilemma of form rather than substance, of a lack of oil for our lamps. At a men's prayer breakfast in our church, a layman reflected on the declining membership of churches across the land, the lack of spirit and vitality that he finds in many places, compared to the vitality that he senses in his own church. But he didn't give the church credit for that vitality—and he was right. The ingredient that determines the power of the church is the Holy Spirit. Too many churches, and too many of our efforts within churches, are devoid of this dependency. We think we can organize ourselves and be successful. We think our human resources will be adequate for the job.

I'm convinced that growth and vitality, power and meaning, the transforming impact of any church, is dependent upon the Holy Spirit. Whenever we forget that, we are things without fuel, and there is no life that comes from us.

How Do We Prepare for Today—and Tomorrow?

Now here I must introduce an unsettling and unnerving truth about the nature of salvation. I pick up a word from Paul's Letter to the Ephesians to state the dynamics of it: "Work out your salvation with fear and trembling."

What is Paul talking about—aren't we saved? Can't we trust the fact that Jesus has saved us? Of course we can. But remember, friends, salvation is a process. We have to keep that process alive, and nobody else can do it for us.

When the five foolish virgins discovered they were out of oil, the first thing they did was ask to borrow oil from their friends. Some might regard the wise virgins as selfish for not sharing their oil, but their responsibility was to light the way for the bridegroom. Jesus was making the point that there are some things we must provide for ourselves. They cannot be borrowed. Too many people try to live on borrowed religion—their parents' religion, their spouse's, their pastor's. But the only faith that will sustain us today and tomorrow and in the time of judgment is our own faith.

We must also realize that what we did to get ready for the Kingdom twenty years ago may not make us ready today. Louis Gizzard, a sophisticate who pretends to be a redneck down in Georgia, writes funny, but probing and challenging columns. There are things about Louis Gizzard that I don't like. I don't like the way he talks about having been married two or three times—as though that's something to continue talking about. But you can't like everything about everybody, so I commend Louis Gizzard to you. He writes books as well as columns. And those books have delightful and attention-commanding titles. One of them is *Elvis Is Dead, and I Don't Feel So Good Myself*. Another is *If Love Were Oil, I'd Be a Quart Low*. Isn't that suggestive? Even judging? If love were oil, I'd be a quart low.

Some of us are a quart low when it comes to having oil in our spiritual lamps. We're depending upon having filled up with oil twenty-five or thirty years ago. We have Bibles, but we refuse to read them. We belong to the church, but the church is not a vital part of our lives—it's an institution we support, but we give little attention and effort to allowing the Christ of the church to shape our lives. Unless something changes, the day may come when, because we've refused to work out our salvation with fear and trembling, the door will be locked and we will be kept from attending the Kingdom banquet.

What do we do while waiting for the Judgment? In Ephesians 6, Paul has a wonderful word about being prepared. He says, "Be strong in the Lord and in the strength of his might. Put on the whole armor of God, that you may be able to stand against the wiles of the devil." Paul then goes on to list vivid images: "Gird your loins with truth . . . put on the breastplate of righteousness . . . take the shield of faith . . . the helmet of salvation . . . the sword of the Spirit, which is the word of God. Pray at all times in the Spirit, with all prayer and supplication. To that end keep alert with all perseverance, making supplication for all the saints." In other words, while waiting for the Judgment we keep oil in our lamps.

Dr. John Claypool told of going to the barber shop with his father. There was an old man in the shop who had shined shoes for many years. On the right side of his huge overalls, he wore a big button that served as an advertisement for his business. The words on the button read, "While you wait—." Many persons did have their shoes shined while they waited for their hair to be cut.

This same man was a fundamentalist preacher on Sundays, and on the left side of his chest he wore a second button that bore witness to his calling. The button read, "Jesus saves!"

One day, John Claypool looked up at the old gentlemen from the barber's chair and saw him face to face. When that happened John beheld both buttons at the same time, and taken together they confronted him with an unexpected message. That same message summarizes this parable on what we are to do while we wait for the Judgment. Those buttons said quite appropriately, "While you wait . . . Jesus saves!"

That's all there is to it—but that's enough. What do you do while waiting for the Judgment? Accept and trust God's forgiveness and grace today. Do today what God requires of you. Live as if today were Judgment Day, because in one sense, it is. And remember, while you wait . . . Jesus saves!

For further reflection:

We have no connected account of a wedding or wedding feast from Jesus' days. However, the numerous fragments from rabbinic literature show that customs differed from district to district. Weddings in Palestine in the late nineteenth and early twentieth centuries included the custom of going with torches to meet the bridegroom. The most common reason for the bride-groom's delay—and we have a 1906 account of a delay until a half hour before midnight—would be failure to reach agreement about the gifts due to the relatives of the bride. Lively bargaining showed honor.

The bridesmaids would wait with burning lamps, because the kind of lamps they had could not be lighted quickly and the bridegroom might appear at any time. The implications of this parable are in harmony with Matthew 5:14-16: "Let your light so shine before men, that they may see your good works and give glory to your father who is in heaven."

Experiencing the parable at a deeper level:

1. Using whatever method you choose (writing, speaking, round-robin in a group setting, music, artwork, acting, other), express this parable as a modern parable. Use contemporary people, settings, and events that correspond to the first-century examples Jesus used.
2. Express the parable using events from your own life that correspond to the events in the parable. What would Jesus say to you?

2. THE POWER OF PERSISTENCE

Ask, Seek, Knock

Read Luke 11:1-13; 18:1-8

A hesitant driver, waiting for a traffic jam to clear, came to a stop on the expressway ramp. The traffic thinned, but the timid driver still waited.

Finally, an infuriated voice came from behind shouting: "The sign says *Yield*, not give up."

The primary actors in the parables we will study in this chapter neither yielded nor gave up. In fact, that really is the lesson of these parables: The Power of Persistence.

Jesus told two parables with almost identical messages about persistence. The stories are different only in their setting. They make the same point. The first story is recorded in Luke 11:5-13. Jesus told that parable just after he had taught his disciples to pray, using the prayer we call the Lord's prayer. We can imagine the parable answering a question from Peter, "Master, should we really bother God with small concerns like our daily bread?" Jesus answered such a thought, spoken or unspoken, with a parable right out of the experiences of everyday life, the parable of the friend at midnight. Both Jesus and his listeners would have enjoyed the humor of this parable.

Once upon a time a traveler arrived at his friend's house at midnight. Perhaps he had been traveling by night to escape the hot sun of Palestine. Perhaps he had been delayed by business, by a mishap of some kind, or by a stop to help someone along the way. In any case, he was not expected, but he knew his friend would give him a place to sleep for the night. The friend, in the best traditions of Eastern hospitality, would not dream of sending a guest to bed without food. However, he was caught unprepared without a crumb in the house. So he went at once to his neighbor's house and began to knock on the door and to call out, "Friend, lend me three loaves [the usual portion for one person]; for a friend of mine has arrived on a journey, and I have nothing to set before him." The neighbor, waked out of a sound sleep, was anything but sympathetic. He and his wife and children were asleep on their sleeping mats in their little one-room house. Maybe the baby had been teething and had just fallen asleep. At any rate, the neighbor said in effect: "What do you mean by waking me up at this hour! Before you know it you'll wake the children too. Go away. I won't get up and stumble around in the dark trying to find loaves of bread for you." Nevertheless, his friend continued to knock and to ask for bread. We can imagine the neighbor saying, "O.K.! O.K.! Don't wake up the whole neighborhood. I'm getting up. I'll get the bread."

The second parable is found in Chapter 18 of Luke's Gospel. It is prefaced by the words, "And he told them a parable, to the effect that they ought always to pray and not lose heart" (18:1). The passage in Chapter 17 that immediately precedes this one is Jesus' answer to a question from the Pharisees about when the kingdom of God is coming. Jesus' answer speaks of times of uncertainty, trouble, and judgment. Though not directly connected, this parable seems to say, *nevertheless*—no matter how adverse the circumstances seem to be—pray and don't give up.

This second story of persistence has no humor about it. It tells of a judge "who neither feared God nor regarded man." A poor widow kept coming to him for justice against her adversary. Since the widow brought her case before a single judge rather than before a tribunal, it was probably a money matter. Perhaps a debt, a pledge, or a portion of her inheritance was being withheld from her. Scripture speaks frequently of the plight of widows, their poverty and the exploitation they too often suffered. This widow evidently had no influence, no one to speak for her, and no money with which to bribe the judge. Yet she kept returning and pleading with him to hear her case. Scripture is very plain about the judge's motive for his action when he finally acted on the widow's behalf. It says that though the judge cared nothing about justice or about the widow, he vindicated her in order to get rid of her. Her persistence wore him down.

In both instances someone—the reluctant neighbor and the unjust judge— did the decent thing because it was less bothersome than doing nothing. Jesus is making a big point, which we're going to come back to as a primary lesson of this parable, that resistance can be battered down by sheer persistence. He also makes the point that if that is true with two not-so-admirable persons, how much more may we expect God to respond to us as we keep our needs before him. We'll come back to that in a moment. Let's glean from the parable some significant truths.

God Is Good

The first important truth that we note has to do with the *goodness of God.* Lodge it in your mind: If goodness is produced by less than righteous, even evil powers, we can expect limitless goodness from God. Note the judge who "neither feared God nor regarded man" nor the grouchy, reluctant neighbor awakened at midnight is to be taken as a picture of God. Yet, at the same time, the goodness of God is underscored by the sharp contrast that is drawn here. So underscore it: If goodness is produced by less than righteous, even evil persons, *we can expect limitless goodness from God.*

Now that's the point. Jesus said it very clearly in the passage recorded in Luke 11:11-13. He set the stage by asking the disciples a question: "Those of you who are fathers, if your son asked you for some fish to eat would you give him a snake, or if he asked for an egg would you give him a scorpion?" Then Jesus made his telling point: "If you then, who are evil, know how to give good gifts to your children, how much more will the heavenly Father give the Holy Spirit to those who ask him!" Matthew records the same saying of Jesus, but with a different ending: "How much more will your Father who is in heaven give *good things* to those who ask him!" (Matthew 7:11).

If goodness is produced by less than righteous folk, even evil persons, we can expect limitless goodness from God. We talk a lot about the mystery of evil; what about the mystery of goodness? We receive daily the gifts of God's grace poured out freely without regard for our merit. God still makes the sun shine on the evil and the good, and the rain fall on the just and the unjust. But even more mysterious is God's Spirit at work bringing good out of the actions of weak, fallible, and sinful human beings. Joseph recognized that mystery when he confronted his brothers, who had sold him into slavery in Egypt. Joseph said, "You meant evil against me; but God mean it for good, to bring it about that many people should be kept alive, as they are today" (Genesis 50:19-20).

In 1954 Harper & Brothers published *Documents of Humanity*, compiled by K. O. Kurth and containing a foreword by Dr. Albert Schweitzer. It was a collection of testimonies from German refugees who were expelled from their homes by the victors in World War II and had to travel, without food or clothing, through what was now enemy territory. Yet these testimonies tell of unexpected kindness, a protection and mercy shown by their enemies. Indeed there were instances where "enemies" actually risked their lives to care for people whose nation's soldiers had invaded their land.

How rarely do acts of kindness, mercy, and generosity become news! We live in a time when newspaper headlines and television news shows are dominated by stories about deceit, selfishness, immorality, corruption, catastrophe, murder, rape, drunkenness, hatred, and suspicion. Through some perverted sense of the dramatic, it is assumed that evil alone is news. This point of view warps our judgment and leads us to the pessimistic view that there is little good left in the world and that few people have the capacity for goodness. To be sure, if we know our own hearts, we cannot deny the existence of evil, but we cannot deny the presence of goodness either.

Where does this come from—this goodness, this decency, this humanity? Does a mechanical theory of evolution account for spiritual qualities such as brotherhood and love? Can a blind, inhuman force create persons who put their duty to their brethren above their own comfort? Shall we assume that evil is a mystery but kindness is automatic? Jesus did not think so and neither do I.

Jesus looked about him and saw the unmistakable signs of God. The marks of a divine origin in His fallen children spoke of a pure source of concern and care. If a man will give his neighbor bread from unworthy motives, how much more may we depend upon the God who is the Father of all? If a judge will vindicate a woman just to get rid of her, how much more may we expect justice from God? If we can never quite escape our hunger for righteousness, what does that say about our

Creator? All of these experiences, says our Lord, bear testimony to the greatness and goodness of God. Rejoice and be glad that through all the changing scenes of our earthly life, we can be sure of God and His care.

Lloyd Douglas had a friend who was a violin teacher, though not a very successful one. But the old man had a good deal of wisdom that was refreshing. Douglas called on him one day and said, "Well, what's the good news today?" The old music teacher went over to a tuning fork suspended by a cord and struck it with a mallet. "There is the good news for today," he said. "That, my friend, is A. It was A all day yesterday. It will be A all day tomorrow, next week, and for a thousand years. The soprano upstairs warbles off-key, the tenor next door flats his high ones, and the piano across the hall is out of tune. Noise all around me, noise; but that, my friend, is A." (*The Parables*, by Gerald Kennedy (Harper & Brothers Publishers, 1960); pages 24–25)

Jesus is telling us something like that in these two parables. You and I are not always good, but God is. Even though our goodness is sometimes produced by the wrong motives, by less than righteous persons, even by evil persons, we can, nevertheless, expect limitless goodness from God.

Sometimes We Are Made Better in Spite of Ourselves

Now there is a second lesson from the parables that is not primary, but it is a lesson well worth paying attention to. That lesson is this: sometimes we're made better in spite of ourselves. The unjust judge didn't want to be good—the reluctant neighbor didn't want to be good—they were made good, or at any rate they did something that was good, in spite of themselves.

My beloved bishop, Gerald Kennedy, under whom I served in Southern California, was one of the most imaginative preachers in this century. He showed me this particular lesson in the parable. He made the point that sometimes we're made better in spite of ourselves as he talked about the ministry. One of the greatest things about the ministry, he said, is that ministers are often made better than they really want to be. We clergy may rebel against the impossible standards and expectations and against the sometimes seemingly unreasonable qualifications and demands that are laid upon us. Still the ministry is forever an encouragement for us to be better than we know we are. I confess this, not with pride, but at times I know I have been better than I really wanted to be because my vocation and the circumstances of my job demanded it.

I know that there are jobs and professions in which there is the constant temptations to lower your standards—but the ministry works just the opposite. The temptation in the ministry—and I'm choosing my words carefully—the temptation is to be better than we think we are, and that's a great thing. And let me say parenthetically, young men and women (or older men and women who are considering a career change), as you listen to God in terms of what God wants you to do and how God wants you to use your life, consider a vocation that will tempt you to be better than you are.

We talk too much about "guilt by association"; we ought to talk more about "goodness or virtue by association." It works both ways. Wise persons will seek the kind of friends who lift them up and encourage them to be their best, to set high standards, and to give themselves unselfishly to others. Our companions rub off on us. Many people can bear witness to the fact that their lives have been lived on a little higher plane than would have been possible had it not been for the example and encouragement of a friend (*The Parables*, by Gerald Kennedy; page 19).

The big point is that sometimes we're made better in spite of ourselves. That's what happened to the judge and to the reluctant neighbor—they didn't want to respond, they resisted, but the pressure of circumstance made them do what was right.

Have you ever reflected upon the fact that that's the reason we have laws— to make us better in spite of ourselves? I remember back during the civil rights movement, supposedly Christian people in the South would bring out the argument that went something like this: "You can't legislate morality; a person's heart must be changed." Of course, there is enough truth in that to deceive us, but it's only half a truth. No one would insist more than I that persons' hearts must be changed. But let it be known, and known clearly, that you can legislate justice and morality—in fact, that's what law is all about.

During the tumultuous days of the civil rights struggle, many of us who are white were made better in spite of ourselves. The dramatic witness of civil rights workers, the commitment that cost many of them their lives, the revelation of the dire conditions under which so many black people were living, the dramatizing of how they were kept by law as nonpersons—all of that made many of us better in spite of ourselves.

At every level of life we find people responding to the circumstances in which they find themselves by being better in spite of themselves. Sometimes a particular office or responsibility brings out our best. Historians have noted that the presidency of the United States has brought out the best in many people. Some of our presidents have been far better than their previous records would have led anyone to expect. And the needs of the moment have led many humble men and women to be better than they had ever expected to be.

Many years ago the steam ship *Halifax* was in a collision at sea, just off the coast of Massachusetts. Fire broke out on board. Many of the crew members deserted their posts. Terrorized passengers leaped into the water. But a deckhand named Lester Kober saved the day. He went into the deserted engine room, where he had no obligation to be, and put out the blaze. During the formal investigation that followed, he was asked if there wasn't a great deal of smoke in the engine room. He replied that there was.

"Didn't you realize that it was dangerous for you to stay there?" he was asked.

"I don't know, sir," he replied, "I was not the judge of that."

"But you stayed, didn't you?"

He answered, "Yes, I did."

And then when he was pressed to say whether he stayed out of a sense of duty or simply because he didn't know what else to do, he replied with quiet dignity, "I saw that someone was needed there" (Barry Boulware, "The Best of All," August 26, 1984).

We can expect limitless goodness from God, and let's remember that *sometimes* we're made better in spite of ourselves.

Pray and Don't Lose Heart

We have yet to come to the core truth of this parable. Neither the judge nor the reluctant neighbor is the central actor in this drama. The spotlight must be kept on the widow and the fellow who had an unexpected guest drop in at midnight. And the lesson centers on persistence . . . the power of persistence. One lesson is specific; the other general. The specific point has to do with prayer. Remember that Luke introduces Jesus' parable of the unjust judge and the persistent widow with this word: "And he told them a parable, to the effect that they ought always to pray and not lose heart" (18:1). The parable of the reluctant neighbor and the friend at midnight immediately follows the request of the disciples to Jesus for him to teach them to pray.

So, Jesus is teaching us about prayer. And I believe he's saying at least three things:

One, sincere prayers are always answered.

Two, persistent prayers are always answered.

Three, prayers that voice our deepest needs in keeping with God's will are always answered.

Let it be noted and underscored that Jesus does not picture either the unjust judge or the reluctant neighbor as a symbol or a metaphor for God. He's not teaching us about the nature of God—he's teaching us about the nature of our praying. Unfortunately, we get confused at that point. That's the reason we must keep our focus clear. *God is the one that we address "Abba, Father." Jesus is trying to teach us about how we should pray, not the nature of the one to whom we pray.* Sincerity, persistence, the voicing of our deepest need, in keeping with God's will. That's what prayer is all about.

And we need that word. Many of us would be embarrassed to knock on a neighbor's door at midnight. But the parable of a friend at midnight tells us that we can call on God at any time. Many of us would be reluctant to admit that we hadn't been prepared for the very small emergency posed by the arrival of just one unexpected guest. Many of us hesitate to pray when we know we are at fault and have not done everything we should have done to remedy the situation. But this parable tells us to ask God's help no matter what we have done or what we have failed to do. Many of us quickly take one *no* or even a *maybe* as a final answer to any request. Both parables we are studying in this chapter tell us to persist, to keep on asking and seeking and knowing until we receive what God is wanting to give us.

As we think about prayer, I think we ought always to keep the emphasis on the affirmation that *prayers that voice our deepest need in keeping with God's will are answered. Prayer gives God a chance to meet our needs.* Jesus said of the reluctant neighbor, "He will rise and give him whatever he needs." And then Jesus sounds that almost unbelievable word, "Ask and it will be given you; seek, and you will find; knock, and it will be opened to you" (verse 9).

Prayer gives God the opportunity to meet our needs. When our grandson,

Nathan, was five months old, it became obvious that he had a sight problem. He couldn't focus his eyes. But his problem was far more serious. A pediatric ophthalmologist pronounced the grave word that Nathan had an underdeveloped optic nerve that medically was not correctable. He used these words to indicate the condition, "The nerve is thin and white and about fifty percent normal size." There were other possibilities for underdevelopment and growth limitations of the eyes.

Our congregation in Memphis went through that trauma with us and sustained Nathan's parents in their loving prayers. Countless people across the land have prayed for Nathan.

When Nathan was nine months old, his family moved from Columbus, Ohio, to Hartford, Connecticut. Instead of waiting until he was a year old to get another examination, as the game plan had been, they took him to the pediatric ophthalmologist at nine months. The doctor couldn't believe the previous diagnosis. Instead of saying the optic nerve is "thin and white and about fifty percent normal size," he said that it's "pink and healthy and is smaller than normal." A conservative diagnosis, he says, is that it may be seventy-five percent normal size; but he thinks it may be just a small nerve on a curve of possible sizes when you are trying to define what's normal.

The immediate conclusion is that the previous diagnosis was a mistake in terms of severity. The previous diagnosis was grave and caused great trauma for the family. It's hard for me to think of a doctor making such a dramatic miscall.

My daughter said she couldn't bring herself to suggest that the first doctor may have been as correct in his diagnosis as the present one—but that God's power, released through the mysterious dynamic of prayer, had been at work.

We're happy today—exhilaratedly happy. At this point it doesn't look as if Nathan's vision is going be limited at all. We are not going to debate medical issues. We're going to continue to thank God for answered prayer and keep on praying, believing that our loving God responds and that our prayers give God the opportunity to meet our needs.

What do you need today? Do you need forgiveness and cleansing from the wrongs you have done yesterday? Do you need strength for a weak will? Do you need forgiveness for opportunities for growth that you have let slip past? Do you need courage to face a tomorrow that fills you with fear? Do you need someone or something to give purpose to your life? Do you need companionship in loneliness and comfort in sorrow? Do you need rest from burdens that have grown too heavy for you to carry any longer? Do you need comfort in grief or pain? Do you have a feeling of inadequacy in the presence of opportunities and obligations that you know you ought to meet? Do you need strength to withstand temptations or courage to dare to grow and to undertake new ventures for God? Whatever our needs, God is eager to meet them if we only give him a chance.

That's the specific lesson of these parables—a lesson about prayer. And especially the lesson that prayers that voice our deepest needs in keeping with God's will are always answered. *Prayer gives God the opportunity to meet our needs.*

When You Are Tempted to Give Up

Now the final and general lesson in the parable is a lesson about persistence. The point is this: *Life demands persistence; life rewards persistence.* We need to remember this truth when we are tempted to give up. Some years ago—maybe ten years ago—*Sports Illustrated* carried a story about the great golfer, Bobby Nichols. Donald J. Shelby retold that story in a sermon.

> When he was seventeen years old, Bobby Nichols was one of five young people crushed beneath a car when it failed to make a curve. The highway patrolman thought Nichols was dead and covered him with a sheet. The doctor called to the scene of the accident looked over all the accident victims and then pointed to Nichols and said, "Don't worry about this one. He won't make it. Let's try to save the others." But Bobby didn't die. Thirteen days later he opened his eyes for the first time since the accident. His injuries included a broken pelvis, a punctured spine, a collapsed lung, a bruised kidney, and damage to the brain—and despite the healing of his body, a damaged spirit that kept him depressed and despairing. He was not sure he wanted to walk again—and there were hours when he did not want to live at all. He was bitter, resentful, and consumed with self-pity.
>
> A friend remembered that Ben Hogan had recovered from a bad auto accident, and he wrote Hogan a letter telling him about the boy. Hogan wrote a letter to the young man which said in part:

I don't know if there is anything I can say to you that will console you mentally or physically since I know you have been through everything. I don't have to tell you that the human body is probably the greatest machine ever known. Given a chance it will heal.

Your determination and will, your desire and persistence at working to get well, doing the exercises and deciding you will get well moves the healing along. As you know, there are no shortcuts—but you can make it.

And somewhere inside his soul, in the silence of night and in the agony of prayer, Bobby Nichols did decide. Ben Hogan could not decide for him. His parents could not decide. It was his decision and his alone. A few days later Bobby sat up for the first time. Later, with great struggle and much pain, he was able to stand on crutches. Later still, he took his first faltering steps. Before long he was swinging a golf club. He entered the University of Kentucky. When he was a sophomore, he won both the conference and the national collegiate golf championships. Later he went on the pro circuit and won twelve major tournaments. ("Mind Your Own Business," September 18, 1977)

The more we know about human psychology and physiology, the better we are able to appreciate Jesus' wisdom in insisting on persistence. How often do we approach the issues of life in a state that could only be described as *half-conscious, half-awake, half-alive, or half-aware*. There may be some things we can do that way, but prayer is not one of them. Jesus spent long hours in prayer wrestling with God's will for his life and seeking the strength he needed to live out that will. Jacob wrestled with an angel at the ford of the Jabbok. David repented and fasted and lay upon the ground all night praying to God for the life of his child. The psalmists cried out to God in praise and lament. The prophets cried out to God in a way that we might come nearer to labeling confrontation than prayer. There seems to be written into the nature of our relationship with God the necessity for us to pray wholeheartedly in order for God to be able to answer our prayers.

The same is true of everything else that is important in life, of everything that we desperately want to achieve, of everything that we hold as valuable. These things do not come to us by *half-conscious, halfhearted efforts—they come through persistence.*

In "The Land of Promise," a pageant written for and given at the 1960 session of the General Conference of The Methodist Church meeting in Denver, there was an especially moving scene. A circuit rider of the frontier days stopped at a running stream for his horse to drink. A stranger came that way and said to him something like this, "Mister, what is it that keeps you always at this?" The circuit rider pondered a moment and said, "Every now and then, some old sinner cracks wide open, and Jesus walks in."

That's the picture—if our commitments are great enough, if what we seek to achieve is important enough, if we really want to be effective in prayer, if we want to be effective in witness, if we want to be disciples worthy of the name of Jesus, we must keep at it—persistence is the key.

The next time you are tempted to give up, remember this: Life rewards persistence—another knock on the door may awaken the reluctant neighbor—another session of persistent prayer may be the key to new understanding, new directions, renewed strength of will, and energizing inspiration—*Life rewards persistence.*

For further reflection:

In a Palestinian village there were no bakeries for buying bread. Each day before sunrise the housewife would bake bread for the family for the day. In a village it would be generally known who would usually have bread left in the evening.

Houses were locked with a wooden or iron bar that served as a bolt, passing through rings in the door panels. Drawing the heavy bolt would make a lot of noise and could easily awaken children sleeping on a mat nearby.

Experiencing the parable at a deeper level:

1. Using whatever method you choose (writing, speaking, round-robin in a group setting, music, artwork, acting, other), express this parable as a modern parable. Use contemporary people, settings, and events that correspond to the first-century examples Jesus used.
2. Express the parable using events from your own life that correspond to the events in the parable. What would Jesus say to you?

3. How to Deal With Demons

The Empty House

Read Matthew 12:38-50

There is an old story about Albert Einstein. He was going around the country from university to university on the lecture circuit, giving lectures on his theory of relativity. He traveled by chauffeur-driven limousine.

One day, after they had been on the road for awhile, Einstein's chauffeur said to him, "Dr. Einstein, I've heard you deliver that lecture on relativity so many times that I'll bet that I could deliver it myself."

"Very well," the good doctor responded, "I'll give you that opportunity tonight. The people at the university where I am to lecture have never seen me. Before we get there, I'll put on your cap and uniform and you will introduce me as your chauffeur, and yourself as me. Then you can give the lecture."

For awhile that evening, everything went according to plan. The chauffeur delivered the lecture flawlessly. But as the lecture concluded, a professor in the audience rose and asked a complex question involving mathematical equations and formulas. The quick-thinking chauffeur replied, "Sir, the solution to that problem is so simple, I'm really surprised you've asked. Indeed, to prove to you just how simple it is, I'm going to ask my chauffeur to step forward and answer your question."

This chapter is not about anything as simple as the theory of relativity. We can learn about relativity with our minds. Most of us could if we determined to do so. This chapter is about something far more difficult—How to deal with demons.

Our parable is one of the most graphic in Jesus' repertoire of gripping stories. It's a story of demons and an empty house.

> In Jesus' day, the belief in demons was widespread. The prevalent cosmology [the understanding of the universe] assigned to God a realm of calm above the sky, and intervening between God's dwelling-place and man's earth was the demon-filled air. A man's most fearful foes pressed about him invisibly. Many sicknesses were but demon-possession [Mark 9:38, and many such references]. Calamities were brewed in the cauldrons of that same grim realm. Paul hints that the malice of the cross was inspired by demonic agency [1 Corinthians 2:8]; and elsewhere he declares that the Christian's hardest battle is "not against flesh and blood but with the angelic Rulers, the angelic Authorities, the potentates of the dark present, the spirit-forces of evil in the heavenly sphere" [Ephesians 6:12, Moffatt]. He warns us of the "prince of the power of the air" [Ephesians 2:2]. Human life in that day was demon-ridden. *We* see the sky filled with light, but *their* sky was filled with unseen malignities. That the Christian faith could conquer the demons and drive them into oblivion is a striking tribute to its power. Jesus alludes to the exorcists who claimed control over the demons [Luke 11:19. The interesting phrase "by the finger of God" in Luke 11:20 probably is an echo of a formula of the exorcists: "I adjure thee by the finger of God"]. Probably the claim was not proved. Not until He spoke did the demons flee. (*The Parables of Jesus*, by George A. Buttrick (Harper & Brothers Publishers, 1928); page 74)

Now we may not have the same understanding of the world and of demons as was prevalent in New Testament times—but few of us would reject the presence and power of the demonic in ourselves and in our world.

So, this is a story about demons. It's also the story of an empty house, in fact we call it "the parable of the empty house." That's an image that grabs our attention because most of us have experienced the sadness of an empty house. A house is left unoccupied for a period of time. Dust gathers. Spiders spin their webs in every corner. The plaster falls off the walls and the paint

36

chips away. Rats and mice have the run of the place. Vermin claim the empty rooms. Left to themselves, unoccupied, empty houses show how things deteriorate when they are not used. Emptiness seems always to be an invitation to vandalism and destruction as well as to the slow decay that sets in upon unattended things. It's that image of the empty house that Jesus uses to teach a lesson about demons. Here is the way George Buttrick describes it:

> A demon is expelled from a man's life. Therefore he wanders, a grisly presence, through "waterless places," seeking rest, but finding none. (For it was supposed that exorcised spirits made their unquiet dwelling in the wilderness or in forbidding ruins [see Isaiah 13:21; 34:14].) He resolves to return to the life from which he was banished. He still calls it "my house" (for evil yields stubbornly), and is overjoyed to find it "empty, swept, garnished." No better tenant had replaced him! Thus he takes new possession of the house; and, lest his tenancy should be again disputed, he brings seven other demons to live with him. [Seven devils was the worst state of demondom. That was why the plight of Mary Magdalene was so desperate. See Luke 8:2.] With these horrible reinforcements he can defy any new attempt to dispossess him. So, says Jesus—clinching the grim story in a sharp proverbial phrase—"the last state of the man becometh worse than the first." (*The Parables of Jesus*, pages 74–75)

The parable is packed with meaning, so let's move through it and garner its message.

The Persistence of Evil

The first, most obvious lesson of this parable has to do with the presence and persistence of evil.

There is an ongoing debate within and outside the church about the nature and presence of evil, or specifically, the nature and presence of demons. Most of us are not prepared to return to a literal, first-century explanation of demons and the work of demons in our life. In that day, almost everything bad that happened to people was ascribed to the work of demons. Demon possession was the primary explanation for physical and mental illness and

37

for unacceptable behaviour. While we are not willing to have that kind of rigid understanding of the world, there is a profound truth in this view of the reality of the demonic, in that it simply underscores the reality of evil.

Psychologists and psychiatrists are joining preachers and theologians in giving credence to a concept of demon possession that gives evil an objective existence of its own. The witness is convincing that we're struggling with more than the consequences of what we have personally willed or caused. Evil is far more than negative good—far more than the consequence we bring upon ourselves by wrong decisions and actions. We are in the grips of forces that defy our power to master. "Even though we may reject making evil an entity that occupies space—a literal, objective evil spirit—we can affirm the existence of evil which is more than the consequences of our actions and by which we are held in bondage" (*Expect a Miracle*, by Roy C. Clark (Discipleship Resources, 1976); pages 38–39).

David Roberts taught at Union Theological Seminary during the 1940's and '50's. Dying in his mid-forties of cancer, he is quoted as saying a few days before his death, "If I ever should become healthy again, I will be able to say what the demonic is." Paul Tillich, who reported these words, remarks that "he was not allowed to, but those who read his sermons . . . cannot fail to recognize that he knew what the demonic is, namely powers in soul and society against which the good will, even of the best of us, is without power" (*The Grandeur and Misery of Man*, by David E. Roberts (Oxford University Press, 1955); page vii).

Do you have questions about the power of evil, the presence of demons in our lives and in the world? An Adolf Hitler, a Joseph Stalin, an Idi Amin ought to be enough to convince us that evil is often incarnated. There are people who have denied the good for so long, have so completely turned their backs on God and on the leading of the Holy Spirit, that evil has become second nature for them. They have lost all sense of guilt for wrongdoing or of responsibility before God and humanity for their actions. They no longer have empathy or compassion. Of their own power they can no longer choose the good.

A system of slavery modernized in South African apartheid ought to be enough to convince us that evil is often institutionalized. The officially sanctioned, or tacitly permitted, torture of political prisoners—and other prisoners—in many parts of the world can only be labeled institutional evil. The same can be said for government policies that prevent the delivery of food and medical supplies to starving people and of a mindset that would seriously entertain the possibility of nuclear or biological warfare. But institutions that do not set out to be evil can inflict great suffering through becoming rigid, callous, and implacable. And men and women can feel helpless to make significant changes in bureaucracies, corporations, and institutions that seem to take on a life and a will of their own.

But most of us can best understand, identify, and deal with evil at the personal level. It's not difficult for us to think in terms of being oppressed by psychological demons. Anger, depression, self-depreciation, greed, suspicion, fear, ambition, anxiety, insecurity—and the catalogue could go on and on and on—a host of demons can invade our lives and defy our efforts to get rid of them. As we struggle with our moods and tempers, our temptations and our exhausting efforts to reform ourselves, we discover the power of forces with which we have to do battle. We're humbled to recognize that we do wrestle against principalities and powers, against forces that are present within us and that are persistent in their effort to control our lives.

In the parable, Jesus reminds us of the presence and the persistence of evil.

The man whom Jesus was talking about did not like the evil spirit that had been living in the house of his life. He wanted to get rid of the wicked thought or emotion that was pestering him. He therefore drove the evil thing out of his life. Not only that, but he also cleaned the place up afterward. This man no doubt was pleased with himself. Now he could live at peace. But his freedom from evil was not long-lasting. Almost before he realized it a plague of other evil spirits came upon the poor fellow. He had not bargained on the persistence of evil.

Not many of us do bargain on the persistence of evil. We get rid of some troublesome evil and tidy up the place; then some other wicked thing comes along. . . . We renounce the lusts of the flesh only to become victims of pride or greed. We get rid of hate only to have worry or fear plague our days. We are too good to steal or murder, but our very self-righteousness catches up with us. We will not tolerate intolerance, but we entertain the selfish spirit almost without knowing it. We think we have successfully buried some deep-set resentment or hatred only to have it come back in some form of mental or physical ailment. We subdue our passions but find them coming to the fore again in our suspicions, jealousies, and ill-temper. We outgrow the sensuality of our youth and discover the materialism of old age.

In this parable Jesus does not attempt to discuss the whole problem of evil. He is describing the tactics of evil desires as they strive for the possession of the human soul. He is saying that the struggle with evil is a lifelong conflict. He is warning us against the stealthy, insidious, persistent attack of evil habits and attitudes against the heart and mind. (*Sermons on the Parables of Jesus*, by Charles M. Crowe (Abingdon Press, 1953); pages 93–94)

The presence and persistence of evil, of the demonic, in our life is very real. Captured dramatically in Matthew 12:44, when the demon had wandered over the waterless places seeking rest, but finding none, he said, "I will return to my house from which I came." How does that grab you? *My* house! The demonic thinks it has ownership; thinks it has a right to reside in our house!

The Empty House

Let's turn from the demons and look at the parable from another direction: *the empty house.*

This parable is very much about emptiness. Scientists often underscore the principle, "nature abhors a vacuum." It's true of the whole of life. The empty mind, the empty heart, the empty life is like an empty house. It is open to whatever demons will come and occupy it. Gerald Kennedy made the point by talking about vacations,

Vacations are fine things precisely because they are limited. They are bound on both sides by work; without those boundaries they would become vast wastelands of despair. An eternal vacation would be a good definition of hell, as Shaw said, while the empty, purposeless days of idleness are more destructive than poverty. A retired man was asked how he was getting along, and he replied that his main problem was insomnia. "I can sleep all right at night and during the forenoon," he said, "but late in the afternoon I just pitch and toss." Pity the retired man whose retirement is nothing but idleness. (*The Parables*, by Gerald Kennedy (Harper & Brothers Publishers, 1960); page 37)

This parable may well be the original inspiration for the folk saying much beloved in times past by teachers who gave long assignments: "The idle mind is the devil's workshop." A certain amount of idleness or leisure, however, can provide the opportunity for creativity. But that is not what Jesus is talking about here. The emptiness Jesus is describing in this parable is a debilitating absence of vibrant life, an apathetic and mindless neutrality, the mistaken idea that goodness is a negative quality, an adherence to "don'ts" rather than a striving for the best.

George Buttrick asked the question, "Can neutrality ever be dangerous?" And for an answer he turned to Jesus' message in this parable: "The answer of Jesus is unqualified: moral neutrality is everywhere in imminent peril. To abstain from self-commitment is not safe; it is beset by danger" (*The Parables*, pages 93–94). This parable then is about moral neutrality, about emptiness. The empty mind, the empty heart, the empty life is like an empty house— open for demons to come and take residence and control us.

We can see the danger of emptiness, of moral neutrality, in some very practical areas of concern. Have you ever heard parents say they're not going to try to bring up their children in the Christian faith because they don't want to indoctrinate them? "Let them decide for themselves what they believe about religion," they say. Parents who have tried that discover too late that their children get their instruction from someone else. Teaching about beliefs will come either from parents who care and understand or from others who may not care and may not understand.

To live is to believe in something and to live by something! A person does not wait until the age of eighteen or twenty-one to need the assurance of God's love, the forgiveness of sin, the opportunity to be a follower of Jesus Christ, the comfort of fellowship with others who love God, the understanding that we are commanded to love one another as God loves us, and the hope of resurrection and eternal life. To think otherwise is to fail to understand either the nature of religion and how persons come to faith or the nature and needs of childhood and youth. Human beings of every age will always look for meaning whether it be through faith in God, through devotion to some self-styled demagogue, or through escape in using drugs. Life fills in every attempt to create a spiritual vacuum, even though we bless the vacuum with the title of "broad-mindedness."

Another area of practical concern is marriage. In marriage, isn't one of the biggest problems emptiness? The space in the relationship is not filled, and demons creep in to divert the relationship and bring it to destruction. It's not enough in marriage to have a good sexual relationship. It's not enough simply to be bound by the mutual responsibility of being parents. It's not enough to have a house, even a big house—and things—even a surfeit of things. Most of us know at least one dramatic story of a wife who, on the surface, was provided everything, it seemed—big house, closet full of clothes, money, car, clubs—everything. Her situation looked perfect, enviable. And then we learned she had become an alcoholic. Her explanation is most often cast in words like these: "I felt empty. I had no meaning. I got tired of all the things, the surface relationship, the superficial glamour; I had to escape." Jesus would appreciate her words; in fact, that's the way it is, not just in marriage, but in all of life he would say. If life is not filled with meaning, demons will come in. The rising tide of alcoholism among women is big confirmation of this truth. And the rage of drug addiction in our nation is further dramatic confirmation. Demons come into the emptiness of our lives. The image of Jesus is vivid and terrifying. Not only did the evicted demon return, he brought seven other demons with him, demons all worse than the first one.

Overcome Evil With Good

That brings us to the third lesson, perhaps the central teaching of the parable. It is captured vividly in what the great Scot preacher, Thomas Chalmers, labeled in his greatest sermon "The Expulsive Power of a New Affection." Neutral living is dangerous, and negative goodness is not enough.

It's not enough just to clean up the house of our life, not enough to evict the demons of bad habits and crippling attitudes. The empty house is especially vulnerable to demons. The person who believes she has just defeated an addiction of some kind may look around her and realize she has hardly begun the task of rebuilding her life. Her addiction has so consumed her that she now finds herself without a job, without interests in life, and without real friends. She is overwhelmed and returns to her addiction more irreversibly than before. We see the same effect in less life-destroying areas of life as well, but it need not be so. The scholar Joachim Jeremias observes that in Semitic grammatical construction we would have a conditional sentence in verse 44 of this parable. The sentence would then read, "*If* he (the demon) on his return finds the house empty." Jeremias goes on to say,

> Hence, the relapse is not something predetermined and inevitable, but something for which the man himself is responsible. The house must not remain empty when the spirit hostile to God has been expelled. A new master must reign there, the word of Jesus must be its rule of life, and the joy of the Kingdom of God must pervade it. (*The Parables of Jesus* (Charles Scribner's Sons, 1963); page 198)

The point is this: Unless we replace what is presently occupying our house with new interests, with positive, active goodness, we are no better off than before. Even more devils will return. Jesus teaches us, not to be overcome by evil, but to overcome evil with good. Howard Thurmond, the great black mystic and champion of the power of the inner life, told a touching story that illustrates, quite literally, and in a very poignant way, the importance of filling our lives with things of value.

One day a somewhat old and weathered man went into a small gift shop on his lunch hour. He was a construction worker. His hands were big and rough and he wore old clothes that were torn and tattered. He just started browsing around and looking at the various items in the shop. One in particular really caught his attention, a very delicate vase made out of beautiful glass and quite expensive. Each day for the next several days, he would come into that shop on his lunch hour just to look at and admire that vase. One day he picked it up and went up to the counter with it.

"Can I put this back on lay away?" he asked the woman at the counter. "I'll be able to pay a little something on it every Friday when I get paid."

And the woman assured him that he could.

Well, the weeks went by, one Friday after another and another. And each Friday, over his lunch hour, that old and weathered man would come into the gift shop and pay a little something on the vase and then leave. And each time, too, he would ask the lady if he could just look at it for a few minutes and hold it. And then the day finally came when the man was able to make his last payment. When he handed the lady his money, and she gave him the vase, she said to him:

"Sir, I've been so intrigued with your love for this little vase and the way you've come in every Friday without fail to pay something on it. If it's not being too nosy, could I ask what you have bought it for?" (And I like what the old man said.)

He replied, "Well, ma'am, I have a small efficiency apartment across town. It's not much, but I decided many years ago that I would furnish it only with the very finest and most beautiful things. You see, ma'am, *that is where I live!*"

As important—maybe more important—than what we don't let live in our house is what we allow to live there. Jesus gave us very clear standards for making choices about how we fill our lives. The commandment that he called the greatest, and the second that is like unto it, are the organizing center of all Christian values and all Christian living:

> "Hear, O Israel: The Lord our God, the Lord is one; and you shall love the Lord your God with all your heart, and with all your soul, and with all your mind, and with all your strength." The second is this, "You shall love your neighbor as yourself." There is no other commandment greater than these. (Mark 12:29-31)

When these commandments become the organizing center of the choices we make and of our attitude toward other people and toward our own life, we have installed good rather than evil at the center of our being. Our house has no room for demons.

Jesus was as psychologically right as any modern student of human nature. There must be an organizing center around which our lives flow. That understanding helps us see that this parable is really a parable about discipleship. Let's go back and note the setting of the parable. It follows Jesus' response to the Pharisees' request for a sign. Jesus refused to give them one, saying, "The sign of Jonah is enough." The people of Nineveh repented at the preaching of Jonah, but something greater than Jonah is here. At the judgment, the people of Nineveh will rise up and condemn those who would not listen when someone greater than Jonah appeared. To underscore his teaching, Jesus called to mind another fact of history familiar to his listeners. "The Queen of the South will arise at the judgment with this generation and condemn it; for she came from the ends of the earth to hear the wisdom of Solomon, and behold, something greater than Solomon is here" (verse 42).

This parable of the empty house speaks in an especially pointed way to the Pharisees who asked for a sign. They had helped to cleanse Israel of idolatry. They were attempting in a legalistic way to eradicate every sin, but Jesus is telling them that they are empty, and worse than empty. Jesus' condemnation of the Pharisees recorded in Matthew 23:25-28 uses images that are akin to the empty house after the seven demons have returned.

> Woe to you scribes and Pharisees, hypocrites! for you cleanse the outside of the cup and of the plate, but inside they are full of extortion and rapacity. You blind Pharisee! first cleanse the inside of the cup and of the plate, that the outside also may be clean.
>
> Woe to you scribes and Pharisees, hypocrites! for you are like whitewashed tombs, which outwardly appear beautiful, but within they are full of dead men's bones and all uncleanness. So you also outwardly appear righteous to men, but within you are full of hypocrisy and iniquity.

Jesus is offering the message of the gospel—a call to repentance more powerful than Jonah's and words of wisdom greater than Solomon's—as the life-giving presence that can fill every empty house, as the power of God incarnate that can cast out every demon. Jesus is calling for commitment to his lordship. He is the one greater than Jonah and Solomon. He is the one God has sent to bring his people back to him through repentance, through forgiveness of their sins, and through lives made new by obedient discipleship—lives surrendered to his lordship.

Jesus tells his parable of the empty house after referring to Jonah and Solomon, then after the parable there is that word of severe clarity—the call to discipleship that you cannot miss. In verses 46-50, Matthew tells that while Jesus was still speaking—still sharing this parable—his mother and his brothers stood outside and desired to speak to him. But he replied to the request, "Who is my mother and who are my brothers?" And then he pointed to the disciples and said, "Here are my mother and my brothers!" Then he adds that very clear word, "For whoever does the will of my Father in heaven is my brother, and sister, and mother."

So this is a parable of discipleship. Jesus is saying that we have to run the demons out of our life, but more, we have to make him the Lord of our life.

We have to allow the Holy Spirit to take residence there, to fill up our lives with meaning and direction, in order that other demons will not return and claim us. It's a matter of the expulsive power of a new affection.

How do we deal with demons? We make Jesus Lord of our life. We allow him to be the organizing center around which our life turns. John knew this truth. In the fourth chapter of the first epistle of John, he wrote about the spirits—the demons that seek to mislead us and to control our lives. He spoke of the spirit of the antichrist, which was powerfully present in the world. The he added that bracing word, "Little children, you are of God, and have overcome them; for he who is in you is greater than he who is in the world" (1 John 4:4).

The struggle is constant, the struggle between the demonic—all that would destroy us and lead us astray and make us less than God wants us to be—the struggle between those powers and the Holy Spirit empowering us as Jesus becomes Lord of our lives.

Toyohiko Kagawa confessed the struggle. He recognized evil in the slums of Kobe, Japan, where he went to live and serve in Christ's name. The devil almost succeeded in undermining Kagawa's soul. Discouragement and despair clouded his vision and he was ready to quit. Kagawa wrote:

> One month in the slums
> > And I am sad,
> > > So sad
> I seem devil-possessed,
> > Or mad . . .
> Sweet Heaven sends,
> > No miracle
> > To ease
> > This hell;
> The careless earth
> > Rings no alarm bell
> Is there no way
> > That help can come?

But Kagawa resisted the devil's temptation to quit, to give up, to compromise his commitment. And later this Christian saint wrote:

Unless thou lead me, Lord,
The road I journey on is all too hard.
Through trust in Thee alone
Can I go on.
(*Songs From the Slums*, by Toyohiko Kagawa (Cokesbury Press, 1935))

How do we deal with demons? Through the expulsive power of a new affection—love God with all our heart, mind, soul, and strength, and loving our neighbors as ourselves—all made possible by God's redeeming love revealed in Jesus Christ. How do we deal with demons? By making Jesus Lord of our lives—"He who is in you is greater than he who is in the world."

For further reflection:

The term "unclean spirit" is the Jewish synonym for "demon."
Seven is the number of perfection. Seven demons would represent all that is evil.

Experiencing the parable at a deeper level:

1. Using whatever method you choose (writing, speaking, round-robin in a group setting, music, artwork, acting, other), express this parable as a modern parable. Use contemporary people, settings, and events that correspond to the first-century examples Jesus used.
2. Express the parable using events from your own life that correspond to the events in the parable. What would Jesus say to you?

4. Good for Nothing

The Barren Fig Tree

Read Luke 13:1-9

The story is told of a man in East Liverpool, Ohio, whose oil well caught fire. The fire was uncontrollable, one of those intense fires that no one was able to put out. Finally, in desperation, the oil well owner offered a three thousand dollar reward to whoever could put out the fire. Well, all the fire companies from the surrounding cities and villages came to the oil well site and tried to put out the fire, but the fire was so intense that no one could get near enough even to attempt to put it out. They had all given up and were just sitting around watching the fire burn when a volunteer fire department from the village of New Calcutta arrived on the scene. New Calcutta was a tiny little place. They had one fire truck, one ladder, three buckets of sand, two buckets of water, and one blanket. They came wheeling into the oil field, and to everyone's surprise, they didn't stop at some distance from the raging fire as the other fire fighters had done. Boldly and bravely, risking the fires of hell, they rolled right up to the blaze—in fact, almost into the blaze—jumped out, climbed their ladder, threw their buckets of water and sand on the fire, smothered it with their blanket, and put the fire out. When the owner of the oil well presented them with their three thousand dollar reward, he asked them.

"How are you boys planning to spend this money?"

They didn't hesitate a minute. As one man they replied, "The very first thing we're going to do is put new brakes on this blasted fire truck."

I tell the story to make the point that "things are not always what they seem," and to introduce our study of the parable of the barren fig tree. This parable is clearly a parable of judgment. But it is also a parable of grace. We'll come back to ways the parable speaks of grace, but let's begin with the obvious.

The Relationship Between Sin and Suffering

The parable is introduced by a question about sin and its consequences asked of Jesus by some people in the crowd. Let me make a dogmatic statement in order to lodge clearly in our minds the truth Jesus taught about suffering: "All affliction is not due to wrongdoing, but all wrongdoing brings affliction" (*The Parables of Jesus*, by George A. Buttrick (Baker, 1973); page 107).

The word of Jesus and the dominant note of the parable is this: "Unless you repent you will all likewise perish" (verse 3).

We will better understand both the parable and the question about sin if we are clear about the historical context of these sayings. In Jesus' day in the Holy Land, Roman legions were a sore provocation to the Jews. On many occasions the yoke of Roman control would chafe so painfully that it would become unbearable. Though they knew that resistance was hopeless, some people at times could stand the burden no longer, and they would hurl themselves against their mighty foe.

One day a certain group came to Jesus, telling him of a gruesome tragedy. Some Galileans were offering sacrifice to God—no doubt they had been protesters against the oppressive rule of Rome. While they were engaged in worship, Roman soldiers slaughtered them mercilessly. The blood of the worshipers and that of the animal sacrifices they were offering mingled together at the altar. It was a horrible sight.

Those telling the story asked Jesus, "Were these Galileans sinners above all Galileans?" The belief of these questioners was that *where there is great suffering there is, of necessity, great sin.* Suffering was regarded as punishment for sin in the faith of most people in that day.

The reporters of the outrage apparently hoped to receive from Jesus an endorsement of their conviction that the victims had induced this violent death by their sins. . . . The theory is inviting—at least to those spared by adversity, for it exempts them from the pain of sympathy and

50

reckons them among the virtuous. No form of self-complacency is more noxious. Jesus meets it with ruthless truth: "Think ye these Galileans were sinners above all the Galileans? I tell you, Nay: but, except ye repent, ye shall all likewise perish."

This comment is not to be construed as a denial on Jesus' part that wrongdoing has tangible consequences. Sin's aftermath of misfortune is too conspicuous to be gainsaid, and Jesus often recognized it in sadness. But He flatly refused countenance to the theory that calamity is necessarily induced by the sins of its victims. Of an instance of affliction so directly traceable as blindness His remark was categorical: "Neither did this man sin, nor his parents." He recognized nature's appalling impassivity which makes her seemingly careless both of vice and virtue. . . . Yet he bade us have confidence in the irrefragable love of God. The apparent strife between God and nature He did not explicitly reconcile. That strife remains. Along with the mystery of sin and of sin's havoc among the innocent it constitutes the heaviest odds of faith. Jesus met those odds at their most diabolical—and conquered. "Be of good cheer: I have overcome the world." (*The Parables of Jesus*, pages 105–107)

To further his argument against his questioners' misunderstanding, Jesus proceeded to quote to them an example of disaster fresh in their memory, a disaster that occurred, not in Galilee, but in Judea.

Eighteen workmen, engaged perhaps in building Pilate's aqueducts, had been buried beneath the falling of a tower at the pool of Siloam. Jesus asked, "Do you think that they were worse offenders than all the others who dwelt in Jerusalem? I tell you, No; but unless you repent, you will all likewise perish" (verses 4-5).

Jesus is very clear that sin does have its consequences, and that's what he's stating in that graphic word, "Unless you repent, you will all likewise perish." What he is doing is clarifying for all of history a very important truth: Calamity is not necessarily the result of sin. Jesus was certain that the rains fell on the just as well as on the unjust. He taught us that the best among us does not escape suffering and misfortune.

So, the beginning word, "All suffering is not the result of sin or wrongdoing, but all sin and wrongdoing bring suffering;" and "Unless you repent, you shall all likewise perish."

Judgment Is Certain

Now—having refuted the notion that suffering is always a direct result of sin, Jesus tells his parable of the barren fig tree to underscore the fact that judgment is certain.

This parable is really a very simple story. A fellow had a fig tree planted in his vineyard. Every year for three years he had come at the bearing season to get some figs from his tree, but every year the tree bore no figs. Therefore, he found the keeper of the vineyard and said to him, "This tree is no good. Every year for three years, I've come seeking fruit but have found none. I'm tired of this barren tree, cut it down. It's not worth the space it occupies. In fact, it's detracting from the vineyard. It's robbing the other plants of the nutrients and the space they need for healthy growth."

There are two ways to look at this parable—both significantly relevant for us.

The Nations Are Judged

The first is to see this parable as referring to the Jewish nation and its fate. Clearly, Jesus had this interpretation in mind, Israel had received the immeasurable bounty of God's mercy, God's grace, and God's favor—not in material things nor in political dominion—but in the rich blessing of national leaders called by God and in unparalleled prophetic guidance. What other nation had been blessed with so noble a succession of spiritual giants? Abraham, Moses, David, Isaiah, Jeremiah, Amos, Hosea, John the Baptist! No land, great or small, in ancient or modern times, can match that array of inspired leadership. Their wisdom, their insight, their courage, and their dedication still guide and inspire those parts of our world that are faithful to the highest ideals of Christianity, Judaism, or Islam. Their call to justice, righteousness, and peace is still the way to the peaceable kingdom our world yearns for.

But Israel had not responded to the prophets—in fact, Israel had persecuted and killed the prophets. Israel had produced no good fruit in character, in a just and merciful national life, or in outreach to others. Nor was Israel's internal barrenness the end of the mischief. God had chosen Israel and given her the ultimate privilege of being a "light to the nations," a suffering servant, but Israel had chosen to interpret God's favor as personal privilege, and as exemption from the judgment of God which would be visited on less favored nations. Even in the face of the witness of history—division, tyranny, exile, and occupation—and in the face of the passionate and dramatic declarations of the prophets, Israel persisted in being blind and deaf, in being unresponsive to Gods message. So Jesus was saying, "Cut the tree down." Israel is under judgment.

What lessons are here for us? Is there a nation on the face of the earth more blessed than we? The natural blessings that God has bestowed upon us are beyond number, and our nation was founded on ideals of freedom and opportunity. No nation in the whole world has been blessed as we have. Yet we have twenty million people in this nation of ours living in poverty. We rank nineteenth in the world in infant morality and twenty-eighth in the mortality rate for black infants. A baby born in Singapore or Hong Kong has a better chance of surviving its first year than a child of any race in the United States. Children represent more than one third of our homeless population. We have a drug culture that could lead to our ultimate demise. Racism still eats away at the soul of our country. The sword of Damocles hangs over our head in the form of a raging national insecurity that keeps us in an arms race that can only lead to destruction.

"We've been reminded dramatically lately of the miraculous founding of this nation as we have celebrated our constitution as a paramount example of freedom. But how long is the Lord going to abide our sinfulness? How long is God going to abide our cynical, self-serving pride? How long is God going to suffer our waywardness, our turning away from his leading? Might not the Lord look down upon this nation so obviously blessed in exceptional ways and ask, "Where is the fruit of the tree that would be pleasing to me?" When might he chop the tree down and leave us to our own destructive destiny?

The Church Is Judged

But not only the nation stands under God's judgment; what lessons are here for the church? Jesus' harshest words of judgment were directed to the religious leaders of his day. The Pharisees, who received the brunt of that criticism, represented the popular religion of the day. They were not so much the religious elite as the respectable religious people of the time, the people who knew they were the right-thinking, righteous upholders of the law.

What about us? We church people of all denominations have fared well in this country. Real persecution has been almost unknown. We have been planted in a favored spot in the vineyard of God.

My own denomination, Methodism, particularly, was raised up by God in the early history of this nation to be the instrument of God to bring righteousness and holiness to the land. At the Christmas conference in 1784, when a little group of Methodists were putting their roots down in this country, the question was asked, "What can we rightfully expect to be the task of Methodists in America?" And the answer came clear and strong, "To reform a continent and spread scriptural holiness across the land."

The Methodist Church became the "most American" of all churches, following the people wherever they went, making sure that the gospel was heard and that the word of the righteous God was always present. There has been a time in America when we had more local churches than there were post offices.

But where is the church now?

It's interesting that Bishop Richard B. Wilke used the figure of the barren fig tree in his book on the state of The United Methodist Church, *And Are We Yet Alive?* The first chapter of that book is aptly titled, "Sick Unto Death." He describes our "dying church" by giving dramatic statistics such as the loss of two million members since 1968—and the fact that our Sunday school attendance was cut in half between 1964 and 1984.

But he also puts our wallowing in the doldrums "sick unto death" in the context of the fact that we are in a Great Awakening in America.

> More interest is being expressed in religion than there has been in a hundred years. The secular media, seemingly surprised, asks questions about religion. Television and newspapers report what the churches are doing, because people want to know. The hunger for spiritual sustenance is everywhere. People pore over the Scriptures. The spiritual vacuum in the land is demanding to be filled. Sin sick souls, suffering

54

souls, struggling souls are crying out for help. But our denomination is not responding as it ought. ((Abingdon Press, 1986); page 27)

Bishop Wilke closes that first chapter of his book by quoting the parable of the barren fig tree and concluding with these words, "God may not have need of the vine called United Methodism in America. He can raise up other groups. Christ will sustain his church and all the gates of hell will not prevail against it. But he can lop off branches that bear no fruit; he can cut down our vine if it fails to produce" (page 28).

That's one way of looking at the parable—seeing it as a call to judgment as it relates to the nation and as a call to judgment as it relates to the church.

We Are Judged

But there's another way of looking at this parable, a more personal way. That perspective also provides challenge. From that focus—the personal perspective—underscore these truths.

One, *unfruitfulness is not allowed in God's vineyard.* Now that's the most obvious truth in the parable, so there is no way to diminish the judgment sounded by Christ, "Cut it down." Unfruitfulness is not allowed in God's vineyard.

You remember that old poem in the vernacular:

> There are a number of us who creep
> Into the world to eat and sleep
> And know no reason why we are born
> Save only to consume the corn,
> Devour the cattle, flesh and fish
> And leave behind an empty dish.

That kind of unfruitfulness is not allowed in God's vineyard.

Flannery O'Connor puts it in a graphic way. She asks the question, "Have you ever looked inside yourself and seen what you are not?" Think about that. Have you ever looked inside yourself and seen what you are not? Well, have you?

What we are not that we should be is what will bring judgment upon us. Unfruitfulness is not allowed in God's vineyard.

What Does It Mean to Be Fruitful?

Now a second focus of the question, "What does it mean to be fruitful as Christians in the vineyard of God?" At least this:

First, that *because of you, the milk of human kindness is readily available to someone.*

Not long ago, I had two or three counseling appointments with a relatively new member of our congregation. This man has fought for a lifetime feelings of worthlessness, guilt, self-depreciation, and failure. He said a surprising thing to me, "For a long time, I have believed in God, but since becoming a part of this congregation, I've come to believe in myself as well as in God."

How did that happen? It happened because people within that church paid attention to him; they simply shared with him the milk of human kindness, which caused him to know that he was worth something. So, that's the first thing that fruitfulness in God's vineyard means: that because of you the milk of human kindness is readily available to someone.

A second meaning of being fruitful as Christians in God's vineyard is that *because of you the spirit of Christ is daily set loose in the world; because of you, persons sense Christ's presence and respond to his grace.*

What does it mean to be fruitful as Christians in the vineyard of God? It means that because of you some person will know there is a Way, a Truth, and a Life that can give them meaning in this life and secure them for eternal life.

My friend, Sir Alan Walker, tells of the Australian poet, Victor Daley, being tenderly cared for in a Catholic hospital as he was dying. One of his last acts was to thank the nurses for all their kindness to him.

"Don't thank us," their leader said, "Thank the grace of God."

Very perceptively the poet asked, "But aren't you the grace of God?"

You see the grace of God is not magical—it doesn't work automatically. It works very practically, and we can trace the course of grace in our lives.

"God so treats us with amazing patience and tolerance that we are predisposed to treat others in the same way.

"God so accepts us that we feel we must accept others. God so forgives us that we are constrained to forgive each other. God so unbelievably loves us . . . that we are inspired to love others" (*Pulpit Digest*, June 1977; page 52).

So—to be fruitful as a Christian in the vineyard of God means *first*, that because of you the milk of human kindness is readily available to someone, and *second*, because of you the Spirit of Christ is daily set loose in the world and persons sense and respond to God's grace.

We've looked at what this parable means as it relates to the nation and the church. We've focused in on what it means to us personally. Now we need to go back to the suggestion made in the introduction, that things are not always exactly as they appear. This parable of the barren fig tree is obviously a parable of judgment—the ringing judgment of Jesus, "Cut it down," is met with the plea of the vineyard keeper. Verse 8:

"Let it alone, sir, this year also, till I dig about it and put on manure. And if it bears fruit next year, well and good."

The worthless tree has its intercessor, and more than a hint of God's grace is here. To be sure there is a law of uselessness that induces death, but there is another law, maybe a deeper law in the economy of God, what George Buttrick called the law of *pitying grace*.

You remember how Abraham nobly interceded for Sodom and how Moses offered his own life with strong tears and utter self devotion for an idolatrous people. And to be sure, we remember Jesus himself hanging on the cross. Can you imagine that even while he spoke the stern warning in this parable, Jesus was getting ready himself to carry his cross, and by his righteous death, to act as the great high priest who pleads the cause for unrighteous people? The note of judgment is at times a final note—but even as that note is sounded boldly, there is that ongoing, heart-touching theme of the gospel, the theme of grace.

Kenyon Scudder, the distinguished penologist, tells this story which was later made into a popular country-western song. A friend of his was riding one day on a train, and seated next to him was an obviously troubled and anxious young man. Finally the boy blurted out that he was a convict returning from prison. His crime had brought shame on his poor but proud family, and while they had written to him, he had refused to see them, so ashamed was he for what he had done.

He went on to explain that he wanted to make it easy for his family. Therefore, he had written them to put up a signal when the train passed their little farm on the outskirts of town. If they wanted him to return home, they were to a tie a white ribbon in the apple tree near the tracks. If they did not want him back, they were to do nothing, and he would stay on the train, go West, and lose himself forever.

Nearing his hometown, the youth's suspense and discomfort grew to where he could not look. Scudder's friend offered to watch, and the two exchanged places by the train window. A few minutes later, the friend had his hand on the shoulder of the young man, who had closed his eyes and bowed his head. The friend whispered in a broken voice, "It's all right! The whole tree is white with ribbons!" (Don Shelby, "Breakthroughs: All the Way Home," March 9, 1986).

"Unless you repent," Jesus said, "You will all likewise perish." That's the resounding note of judgment—but the plea comes, "Give it another year"—the plea of grace; and for sure, because Christ is all grace, grace will be his response—if—if we repent and seek that second chance.

For further reflection:

Jesus' listeners may have been familiar with a folk-tale known since the fifth century B.C. in which a father compared his son to a tree that bore no fruit even though it was planted beside water. When the tree's owner came to cut it down the tree said,

"Transplant me, and if even then I bear no fruit, cut me down."

But the owner replied, "When you stood by water you bore no fruit, how then will you bear fruit if you stand in another place?"

In Jesus' parable the gardener who intercedes for the tree says he will "dig about it and put on manure." This practice is not mentioned in the Old Testament. Fig trees require little care; therefore the gardener is taking the last possible measure in the hope that the tree will bear fruit and be allowed to live.

Experiencing the parable at a deeper level:

1. Using whatever method you choose (writing, speaking, round-robin in a group setting, music, artwork, acting, other), express this parable as a modern parable. Use contemporary people, settings, and events that correspond to the first-century examples Jesus used.
2. Express the parable using events from your own life that correspond to the events in the parable. What would Jesus say to you?

5. SERENDIPITY

The Treasure and the Pearl

Read Matthew 13:44-46

My wife is a clown! Wait now—let me explain that. I mean that *literally*, not *figuratively*. I don't mean she's a clown in terms of being a cutup, an always-clowning-around-type of person; she's that sometimes, not always. *I mean she is literally a clown*, and she has been involved for about ten years now in a clown ministry. She's not very active at present in that ministry, but she has trained a group at our church, and we have a clown troop that is often involved in ministry—in nursing homes, in some of the projects downtown, and at the prison.

Jerry's clown name is "Serendipity," a name given her by a longtime preacher friend in Southern California. One thing the name means is "unexpected" and "unsuspected." The fellow suggested the name because God's grace comes at unexpected times from unexpected sources—even through a clown. The parables we will consider in this chapter are about the unexpected, about serendipity.

One of my favorite preachers, Wallace Hamilton, introduced me to the word *serendipity* twenty years ago. I don't know that I had ever heard it before then—but I heard him preach a sermon on that theme, and then he wrote a book by that title. The dictionary defines serendipity as *the ability of finding valuable things unexpectedly*, or *the gift of finding valuable or agreeable things not sought for*. The word was coined by Hugh Walpole in allusion to a fairy tale entitled "The Three Princes of Serendip," because the three princes were always finding the unexpected. Thus the evolution of a word—serendipity—the ability or gift of finding valuable things in unexpected places.

Jesus didn't know that word, but he knew the truth of it. Listen to him: "Seek ye first the kingdom of God, and his righteousness, and all these things shall be added unto you" (Matthew 6:33, KJV).

Now the word *serendipity* is not too common, but we use it from time to time—usually referring to something good that has happened to us unexpectedly, something extra we had not been looking for.

On our study leave recently, Jerry and I had a serendipity. After a long day of work, we decided to drive to New Smyrna Beach, about an hour away from where we were staying at Orange Lake below Orlando. Jerry grew up going to New Smyrna Beach with her family. It's one of the most treasured memories of her childhood. When we got married, we went to New Smyrna Beach on our honeymoon. Back then it was rather an isolated place, a beautiful, beautiful beach, good food, and not a lot of people around—an ideal place for a honeymoon. At New Smyrna we were in a lovely motel right on the beach.

Well, on study leave we went back to New Smyrna—on a lark—and we found that motel where we had stayed on our honeymoon. What I remembered it as having been then is worlds apart from what it is now. None of you would want to stay now in that motel where we stayed thirty years ago. The serendipity was running upon the motel again and reliving some of those exciting days of our early life together, even finding the little house in which Jerry's family often vacationed when they went to New Smyrna, and having coffee in the Riverside Hotel—an old, old hotel on the river in New Smyrna that has been redone into a very elegant place where, in contrast to the motel, any of you would be delighted to stay.

Serendipity, *something good that happens to us unexpectedly, a grace that comes to us from some unsuspected source.*

The first parable we are considering is about serendipity. Inspired by Clovis Chappell, let me tell the story in a fuller way than the Scripture account, though granted with some imagination.

The Treasure in the Field

Many years ago a very wealthy man in Palestine heard that an army was about to invade his country. The enemy was one of the great powers of the world, and his nation had few defenses. The rich man was afraid the countryside would be overrun by enemy troops, looting and burning. He didn't want the invading army to find his wealth and take it, so he went about the task of hiding his treasure. There were no banks in that day in which he could deposit his money, no lock-boxes in which he could hide it away. So in the dead of night he slipped out and buried his treasure in a field not far from his house.

The conquering army came. They took many of the people captive, including this very wealthy man, and carried them all into exile. There the man died, and the secret of his buried treasure died with him.

The years slipped by—perhaps a generation or two. Now a farmer is cultivating the very field where that treasure had been buried. The farmer is a poor man—too poor to own the land. He's more like a tenant farmer. He's had it hard all his life. For him, life has been dull and boring—a treadmill where he has to keep up a rapid pace day in and day out just to stay even. His days are commonplace and his toil a drudgery. For the most part, hope and expectancy have died. There's no light in his eyes anymore, no spring in his step. No one could convince him of a silver lining behind every cloud.

On this particular day, he faces the same routine. He rises before the sun is up in order to get in a full day's work. And once again, he's doing what he has done so often, following his oxen down one dull row after another, breaking up the field for spring planting.

This day is like any other day, and the farmer has never heard about serendipity. Suddenly his plow scrapes against something, and he is angry. He thought he had gotten all the troublesome rocks out of the field, but here is another. As he scratches around at the rock to throw it aside, he finds there is a shimmering mark on the object, and he realizes that this is not rock, but metal. And as he looks more closely, he discovers that the metal is a part of a chest. The chest has been buried there for perhaps fifty or a hundred years; therefore its hinges and its lock have been weakened. The man's heart is now in his throat. His body is quivering, a light has come into his eyes, his hands tremble as he lifts the loosened top off the chest and takes a look.

63

What he sees is unbelievable—it can't be—he must be dreaming. All glittering in the sunlight is a heap of gold and silver and precious jewels.

He is bewildered as well as excited. What is he to do? He quickly covers the treasure over again, goes to the side of the field and gets a rock to mark the place, and leaves immediately.

He gathers everything he has that is of any value and begins to go from place to place to sell it all. And when he has done so, when he has sold everything he has, he takes the money and goes and purchases the field that he has been tending laboriously through the years.

That's the story, and the central lesson is clear. Jesus says that's what the Kingdom is like. *You will sell everything you own to possess the supreme worth of the Kingdom.* You can't put a price tag on the Kingdom. Whatever it takes to enter, whatever cost may be exacted from us, the kingdom of God is worth it. To enter the Kingdom is the end toward which all life moves. We'll come back to that idea, but there are some other important truths to garner before we get to that point—truths that revolve around the idea of serendipity.

The Best Things in Life Are Serendipities

First, a bold assertion: *Many of the finest things in life are serendipities.* Isn't that true? Now I know there is another side of the coin, and I preach a lot about it: discipline, setting goals, having a purpose, being tenacious and persistent. There are things we get by action, "going for the gold"—but let's not forget the serendipities, those things that come to us by indirection. *We're looking for one thing and we find another.* Many of the finest things in life are serendipities.

Have you experienced this truth? Happiness is not something you find by seeking it, not something you gain by striving for it; it's a by-product, it comes to us by indirection. That's what Jesus was saying: "Seek ye first the kingdom of God and his righteousness, and all these things will be added unto you." That's what Jesus' beatitudes are all about. "Blessed are those—happy are those—the peacemakers . . . , the poor in spirit . . . , the merciful." Their happiness is a by-product of what they're doing, how they're living, the attitudes of their lives.

Think for a moment. What yields you real joy and happiness?

—The spontaneous hug and kiss of your three-year-old? You can't buy that.

—The son or daughter at graduation from high school or college moving proudly into another phase of this wonderful saga of life, and the deep satisfaction of parents—the sigh of joy—we've made it another step? No price tag on that; it's a by-product.

—The thank-you from a friend to whom you've given a cup of cold water when you knew he was weary, and the heavy weight of emotion in his words when he said, "I could not have made it without you"? That's merchandise of the spirit, which can't be bought or sold.

Well, the point is made, isn't it? Many of the finest things in life are serendipities.

Expect the Unexpected in God's Kingdom

A great many of God's actions in the world could be described as serendipities. One truth the New Testament makes clear is that God acts in unexpected ways. Those who heard the gospel message found valuable things unexpectedly. Like the farmer in Jesus' parable, they found treasure where they had expected to find nothing of value: "Can anything good come out of Nazareth?" Some received life's greatest gift even though they were not looking for it.

Jesus was born in a manger, not in a king's palace. Angels announced his birth to shepherds, not to royalty. Jesus called fishermen, not scholars; tax collectors, not rabbis, to be his disciples. He associated with sinners. He said that the first shall be last, and the last first. Jesus taught that the things of real value in life are freely available to everyone: love of God and neighbor; God's providence that clothes the grasses with glory, provides for the birds, and accounts for every hair on our heads; God's grace that forgives our sin, heals our brokenness, and brings us to new birth and new life. Those who could not hear the good news were the ones who wanted to control God, who refused to see God's action in the unexpected.

Serendipities Come to Those Who Are Open

That insight leads to another truth. Serendipities can come only to those who are open, to those who are alive to the moment and who respond to what life is offering now. The farmer was not searching for treasure, but he had the ability to recognize its value once he had found it.

A closely related truth is this: Serendipities come most often to those who believe there is treasure to be found. Hans Christian Anderson's approach to his life and work illustrates this point.

After six weeks away from Denmark, Hans Christian Anderson wrote his book, *Shadow Pictures*. His critics were scornful, "It would take an Anderson to write a travel book after six weeks abroad!" They forgot that he had once made a whole book out of a walking trip across Copenhagen, the city in which most of them had lived all their lives and still had not really seen what a remarkable place it was. In his writings Anderson brought things alive: Darning needles, tin soldiers, pots and pans, fir trees. His critics didn't like him, and nothing he did pleased them. They pounced on every petty thing they could find to criticize. But Anderson's greatness and the power of his imagination is revealed in one such confrontation.

"Here is an error," said one of his critics. "Why do you write dog here with a little 'd'?"

"Because I'm writing of a little dog," said Anderson. Is it any wonder that he has thrilled children for generations! If we will cultivate the wide-eyed wonder of the child, the poet, and the artist, God's kingdom will surprise us with its treasure. Jesus himself said, "Truly, I say to you, unless you turn and become like children, you will never enter the kingdom of heaven" (Matthew 18:3).

I remember a serendipity experience in Hong Kong. Jerry, my wife, and I were walking through a park in one of the resettlement areas. Children were swarming about, playing in the fountains, skipping and running in release from the confines of the restricted twelve-by-fourteen-foot cubicles in which they lived. Among all these children, Jerry saw one child, a little girl asleep on a park bench. No grown-up was around. The child must have been only three or four, wearing just a little blouse for clothing.

This sleeping child was a "burning bush" for Jerry, a serendipity, and she turned aside to see. One of her best paintings was done after our return from the trip. In the foreground, barely visible, are the sampans, then the miserable shacks that have provided the hovel homes of thousands. Dominating the painting are the tall resettlement complexes built by the government and other concerned agencies to provide homes for the thousands who came to Hong Kong as refugees and through the years had lived in filthy misery. A part of the painting is shadowy and dim, but the clouds are breaking in the background and the sun is barely bursting through. It's a lively painting, but a first look reveals no human life. Looking closely though, you see the vague outline of a person. Looking more intently, you discover that the person is a little child lying on a park bench asleep.

For Jerry this was the message of Hong Kong: that little child. "Inasmuch as ye have done it unto one of the least of my brethren, ye have done it unto me" (Matthew 25:40, KJV). Every time I think of my ministry, the ministry of the church, our call to be servants of the world, Jerry's painting looms on the screen of my consciousness. And all because she "turned aside to see."

God's kingdom comes to us, not when we try harder, but when we look closer. Jesus said the Kingdom is in the midst of you—the Kingdom has come upon you. That means we don't work to achieve it. We look for it and receive it when we, like Moses at the site of the burning bush, "turn aside to see," when we give life our attention, when, like children, we hold on to the belief that there is joy waiting to be discovered. Jesus called that joy the kingdom of God.

So remember this: Serendipities can come only to those who are open, who are alive to the moment, and who respond to what life is offering now.

God's Kingdom Is Worth Our Lives

Now we come to the heart of the parable—the surpassing worth of the Kingdom. Jesus told another parable, "The Parable of the Pearl of Great Price," recorded by Matthew immediately following the parable of the buried treasure. You remember the story. A rich merchant was on a continual search for goodly pearls. One day he found the most treasured pearl in all the world, the most beautifully perfect pearl he had ever seen. And he went out and sold all that he had—all of his other pearls included—and bought that one pearl, the pearl of great price. Like the farmer who found the treasure in his field, the merchant did not hesitate to sell all he owned. For him the value of the pearl was so great that parting with everything else was no sacrifice.

Now there is a secondary truth to this parable that we should not miss: *We are likely to find what we search for persistently. We are likely to receive what we want passionately.* Scripture, folk tales, and popular wisdom support this truth. As children we all heard stories about three wishes being granted, sometimes with disastrous results. Our literature is enriched by epics about dedicated souls who searched tirelessly for the golden fleece and for the holy grail, and whose search was rewarded in the end. We know the popular saying, "Be careful what you want because you may get it." And we remember that Jesus said, "Where your treasure is, there will your heart be also" (Luke 12:34).

The life of John Wesley, the founder of Methodism, illustrates this truth. Wesley wanted the assurance of God's presence and God's grace that he saw in the Moravians with whom he had traveled to America. For years he sought God's will for his life in a rigorous prayer life, getting up at four in the morning to pray. He participated in Christian service to those in need, in public worship, and in study. Finally, on May 24, 1738, John Wesley went reluctantly to a prayer meeting in Aldersgate Street. There his long search was rewarded as he heard someone read Martin Luther's preface to Paul's *Epistle to the Romans*. Later Wesley wrote, "I felt my heart strangely warmed. I felt I did trust in Christ, Christ alone, for salvation and assurance was given me that he had taken away my sins, even mine, and saved me from the law of sin and death." The assurance and new life that John Wesley found was impetus for a revival that brought hope and new life to eighteenth-century England and to the American frontier. *We are likely to receive what we want passionately.*

Now back to the central point of these parables. Why did Jesus tell two parables at the same time with the same message? He didn't want anyone to miss the point. The poor and the rich receive the Kingdom the same way—by making it the priority of their lives. And the reward of the Kingdom is the same for both—the poor, plodding plowman who has nothing, and the successful merchant who has everything are both given what they most desperately need.

Jesus says the kingdom of God is like that. We receive the Kingdom and we live in the Kingdom only as we make it the priority of our lives.

> Our danger is that we may partly believe in the treasure, but not enough to act upon our belief. We are not far from the Kingdom at any time, but as long as we are not within it we might as well be far from it. For finally we must choose, we must act. The existentialists are right when they put decision at the center of human experience. If I see the treasure but dare not sell all that I have to buy it, the very experience is but one of frustration. Martin Buber said: "And if there were a devil it would not be one who decided against God, but one who, in eternity, came to no decision."

Is there any hope for those of us who halt between two opinions and make no decision? Yes. For the God who gives the vision will give us also the power to follow it, if we ask Him in faith.

There is an old story about a social worker who could not get a slovenly family to clean up its house. One day she brought a beautiful plant and left it in the living room. It was such a contrast to the room that the family cleaned it up. That made the other rooms look so filthy that they could not stand it and so they cleaned the whole house. Then the outside looked so run-down they decided to paint it and improve the yard. Pressure could not get any result, but a little beauty that opened the family's eyes worked a miracle.

This is the way God works. This is the nature of the Kingdom of God. This is the method of Christ. He shows us a treasure, and in our desire for it we find the meaning of our life and the redemption of our souls. (*The Parables*, by Gerald Kennedy (Harper & Brothers, 1960); pages 212–13)

I leave you with two stories and particularly with two sentences from those stories.

The first comes from many centuries ago. There was a time when the land of Scotland was inhabited by a people known as the Picts. They were a fierce and warring people. They got their name from the fact that they painted or tattooed their skins. They fought the Romans fiercely for many years, and the Romans built two long walls to keep the Picts out of the province of Britain. One day a Christian missionary came to the king of the Picts and told him about Jesus Christ. After hearing something of the story, the king asked what he could expect if he accepted Jesus. The missionary answered, *"If you can accept Jesus, you can expect wonder upon wonder, and every wonder true."* And to that I say, Amen—and thanks be to God.

The second sentence comes from our own century. My preacher friend Ellsworth Kalas tells that when he was in his twenties, five young men about his age went as a missionary team to the Auca Indians of South America. It was a daring venture, for the Aucas were virtually unknown, except for their fierceness. The five young men were slain before their work was hardly begun.

One of the young men was Jim Elliott. When he was a college student preparing to go to the mission field, he wrote down many of his deep convictions. One of his most memorable sentences goes like this: *He is no fool who gives up what he cannot keep in order to get that which he cannot lose.*

Well, Jim Elliott lived by his own word. He gave up what he could not keep: his life—for none of us, ultimately, can keep our lives, you know—in order to get what he could never, never lose: eternal life in Jesus Christ (J. Ellsworth Kalas, "You Bet Your Life," February 8, 1987).

The Kingdom is like that, said Jesus. It will surprise you with its joys and riches, coming as serendipities. But to enter and live in the Kingdom requires that we make it the priority of our life.

For further reflection:

Stories about hidden treasures and valuable pearls were favorite themes for stories in Jesus' day. His listeners would have expected the finder of the treasure to build a splendid palace or to marry a rich man's daughter. The finder of the pearl might discover that the pearl could save his life when he fell into the hands of robbers. However, Jesus surprised his listeners with a different conclusion to his stories.

Experiencing the parable at a deeper level:

1. Using whatever method you choose (writing, speaking, round-robin in a group setting, music, artwork, acting, other), express this parable as a modern parable. Use contemporary people, settings, and events that correspond to the first-century examples Jesus used.
2. Express the parable using events from your own life that correspond to the events in the parable. What would Jesus say to you?

---

6. HOW TO ESCAPE BEING POSSESSED BY POSSESSIONS

The Rich Fool

Read Luke 12:13-34

The parable of the rich fool is one of those parables of Jesus that too many of us dismiss out of hand, thinking it has nothing to say to us because it's about a rich man—a rich man whom Jesus called a fool. But in terms of the population of the world, we are all rich. Furthermore, when we look at the occasion that led Jesus to tell this parable and at the teachings that follow it, we see a message that applies to every one of us—to rich and poor alike.

Once when a great crowd had gathered around Jesus—"so many thousands of the multitude . . . that they trod upon one another"—a younger brother confronted Jesus and said, "Bid my brother divide the inheritance with me." The older brother evidently preferred to keep the family inheritance intact, not giving the younger brother a share. This younger brother was so preoccupied with his own concerns and his own sense of being ill used that he didn't hesitate to bring up a family matter in a crowd of thousands. Jesus' response says in effect, "Don't spend your time and concern on trivial matters that have no lasting significance." Verse 15 reads, "Take heed, and beware of all covetousness; for a man's life does not consist in the abundance of his possessions." That's the way the Revised Standard Version has it. Listen to Phillips: "Be on your guard against covetousness in any shape or form. For a man's real life in no way depends upon the number of his possessions." *The Living Bible* offers a very practical and piercing edge in its paraphrase of this verse: "Beware! Don't always be wishing for what you don't have. For real life and real living are not related to how rich you are."

Do you see? The parable is not about how much we possess, it's about how we feel about what we possess. It's about priorities.

A Parable About Priorities

Charles M. Crowe tells a masterful story about priorities. A man named James McClusky died in New York some years ago. His will left a large fortune to a brother in Scotland, a farm laborer. An attorney for the estate went to Scotland to look for McClusky's brother John. Every one in the countryside knew him. For forty years John had worked at lowly jobs, but he had a reputation for integrity. The lawyer found him slicing turnips for food for the sheep. After identifying himself, the lawyer told John McClusky that his brother James and died and left him a large fortune. Would he come at once and sign the papers? Replied the Scotsman: "I'd talk to ye at 6 o'clock, yong mon. I be workin' till then. Thay fortune will keep, but thay turnips will not" (*Stewardship Sermons* (Abingdon Press, 1960); pages 116–17).

This parable is about priorities. It's about how we feel about what we have. It's about what we put first in life. It's about who or what we trust for our ultimate security.

In this parable Jesus paints a vivid picture of the rich man's priorities. In the three sentences that are a direct quotation from the rich man himself, he uses the word *I* six times and the word *my* five times. His focus is completely upon himself and his possessions:

> He had no thought of God. "*My* fruits," he called them; "*my* grain." But in what sense were they his? Could he command the sap in the tree, the fertility in the soil? Were the sunrise and the sunset under his control? Was the faithfulness of returning season his merit? If the rain had been withheld, where then would have been his wealth? "The *ground* brought forth plentifully"; all the man could do was to take nature's tides at the flood. He was carried to fortune on a fecundity, a light, a heat, a constancy in nature's cycles, which are boundless mysteries of blessing—and he called them "mine"! His title was earned—"Thou fool!" (*The Parables of Jesus*, by George A. Buttrick (Baker, 1973); pages 130–31)

Notice how the parable ends. Jesus condemns the "rich fool," then brings us all into the realm of judgment, verse 21: "So is he who lays up treasure for himself, and is not rich toward God."

None of us are excluded from this sharp and challenging teaching of Jesus. We're talking about a danger common to all of us as we ask the question, "How do we escape being possessed by our possessions?"

Anyone Can Be Victim of a Covetous Spirit

In seeking to answer the question, I want first to sound two reminders. First, *any one of us can become a victim of a covetous spirit.* Sometimes those who don't have much are more covetous than those who do. Indeed, many relatively poor people are greedy at heart. Many rich people realize the emptiness of riches alone. They sometimes escape from covetousness by using their goods in the service of God and humanity.

Jesus' words that follow the parable of the rich fool are addressed to the disciples, who had never been rich to start with and who had given up their ordinary means of livelihood in order to follow Jesus. In those words he cautioned them not to be anxious about possessions. Jesus realized that one of the dangers of anxiety is the way in which it can be used to justify a covetous spirit.

Values in Life Are Not Measured by Material Things

Now the second reminder. *Values in life are not measured by material things.*

Someone has said that money can't purchase happiness, but it can enable you to look for it in some very interesting places. A very wealthy man who has amassed a tremendous fortune at a young age asked his wife one evening, "Honey, would you still love me if I didn't have all this money?" She replied, "Certainly I'd love you, Sweetie; I'd miss you, but I'd love you."

Values in life are not measured by material things. In the Franklin County Courthouse in Virginia, the will of the man who owned Booker T. Washington is preserved. Since most of his property was in slaves, the owner had listed them and set down the price of each one of them. Opposite the name of Booker Washington he had marked, "$200."

Was this a fair estimate of that youngster's worth? He turned out to be one of America's great men. Can any human life be valued in terms of money? Those who so value human beings have themselves suffered a devastating warping and shriveling of their values, their moral sense, and their very spirits. Values in life cannot be measured in material things.

How easy it is to misplace values—not only in relation to material things but in the whole of life. Each of us has to answer in our own hearts as to what we place first. I confess to you that there are temptations that are peculiar to the ministry—to my vocation—that would threaten to pervert ambition and center it not in the kingdom of God but in ourselves. I wrestle with that temptation almost daily.

One of the great preachers of this century, one-time minister of Riverside Church in New York, D. Earnest T. Campbell, tells that for many years during his ministry he kept a quotation tacked on the door of the closet where he kept his robe. On Sundays as he slipped into the robe, he would read those words. They were words copied from Hugh Walpole's *The Cathedral*.

The words were written by a black-sheep member of the cathedral by the name of Davray, to Brandon, a rather pompous clergyman who took himself too seriously. Davray was emboldened by drink one night when he made his way into the cathedral, came face to face with Father Brandon, and said,

> I've been waiting for this moment for years. You don't know how I've watched you Sunday after Sunday strutting about this lovely place, happy in your conceit. Your very pride has been an insult to the God that you pretend to serve. I don't know whether there's a God or not . . . but there is this place, alive, wonderful, beautiful, triumphant, and you've dared to put yourself above it. (*The Cathedral*, by Hugh Walpole (George H. Doran Company, 1922); page 61)

You see, it's easy to misplace values, not only in relation to material things, but in the whole of life.

So we have two reminders: First, any one of us can become a victim of a covetous spirit; and second, it's easy to misplace values and put self in the center of things.

Where Do I Place My Security?

Now let's look at five questions that will give us perspective as we seek to escape being possessed by our possessions. The first question: Where do I place my security?

Our Lord is quite explicit in the suggestion he makes in this parable. *To possess wealth gives one a false sense of security.*

> The rich man in the parable is an illustration of this [the false sense of security that can come from our possessions]. When his ground began to bring forth plentifully, he took an inventory of his possessions and found them enormous, almost embarrassing, and he began to say to himself, "At last I can be at ease." When he surveyed his balance sheets, and looked over the huge new barns he had built and the enormous stock he had laid up, he said to himself, "Soul, thou hast much goods laid up for many years: take thine ease, eat, drink, and be merry." How secure he felt, and how settled he considered himself! He did not need God now; he did not need prayer; for he had so much else. He did not think of the possibility of death and then the judgment seat; he had so many pleasant things to absorb him. (*Many Things in Parables*, by Ronald S. Wallace (Harper & Brothers, 1955); page 146)

Have you ever thought of this way? We envy people who are rich; Jesus pitied them. When we hear of people inheriting fortunes or winning sweepstakes, we think how lucky they are. We think of the freedom from anxiety that wealth could bring, of the marvelous things we could buy, of all the good we could do. Most of us believe that it is good to be rich. We've come to equate affluence with the American dream.

In contrast, Jesus taught that we should beware of riches. (And let's face it. By the standards of Jesus' day, or measured against the world as a whole, most of us have riches.) Matthew, Mark, and Luke all quote Jesus' words, "How hard it will be for those who have riches to enter the kingdom of God! . . . It is easier for a camel to go through the eye of a needle than for a rich man to enter into the kingdom of God" (Mark 10:23, 25).

Luke's Gospel in particular highlights Jesus' teachings about wealth. Beatitudes in Luke's Gospel have different wording from those in Matthew and they are followed by "woes." "Blessed are you poor, for yours is the kingdom of God," and "Woe to you that are rich, for you have received your consolation" (Luke 6:20, 24). "Blessed are you that hunger now, for you shall be satisfied," and "Woe to you that are full now, for you shall hunger" (Luke 6:21, 25). This parable of the rich fool and the parable of the rich man and Lazarus (Luke 16:19-31) appear only in Luke's Gospel. They are designed to show how riches and good fortune in life tend to lead, not to blessing, but to tragedy.

The concern expressed in these teachings is not that the rich got their wealth dishonestly or by oppressing others or that the poor suffer because the rich do not help them. No, Jesus is warning about the deadly peril of trusting in riches for one's security. His concern is for the rich. To seek wealth is foolish and dangerous because wealth has no real value. Wealth can stand in the way of entering the kingdom of God.

The words that follow the parable of the rich fool state clearly where we need to place our security: "Therefore I tell you, do not be anxious about your life, what you shall eat, nor about your body, what you shall put on. . . . Your Father knows that you need [these things]. Instead, seek his kingdom, and these things shall be yours as well" (Luke 12:22, 30-31). Verses 32-34 show that God's promise is not centered in material things, but in the Kingdom, suggesting that the wise and safe thing to do with riches is to give them away.

> Fear not, little flock, for it is your Father's good pleasure to give you the kingdom. Sell your possessions, and give alms; provide yourselves with purses that do not grow old, with a treasure in heaven that does not fail, where no thief approaches and no moth destroys. For where your treasure is, there will your heart be also. (Luke 12:32, 34)

So we need to ask, "Where do I place my security?"

Do I Include God in My Planning?

The second question is closely related to the first: Do I include God in my planning?

When we take God into our planning, we immediately become aware of the fact that all we have—including our time, our energy, and our abilities—

are, in one way or another, a gift from God and that we use those gifts as good stewards. We also become aware of God's concerns, and that leads us to appreciation, love, and concern for other people.

In speaking about the rich fool, George Buttrick observed:

> Of course he was bereft of fellow feeling. Other men had enriched him; for he did not plough, reap, and build barns single-handed. Always wealth is more an achievement of society than of the individual. Society maintains and enforces laws without which separate industry would be impossible. Society provides the bulwark of common honesty which, in the last resort, is the only guarantee of investments. . . . The rich man reached affluence mainly by reason of the commonwealth. Yet he had no gift of sympathy. "What shall I do, because I have not where to bestow my fruits?" Was there no sickness to heal, no nakedness to clothe? Were there none on whom a sharper problem pressed, who were compelled to ask, "What shall I do, because stark poverty has become our guest?" Deliberately this man proposed to spend the rest of his days on the pleasure of his body: "Soul, thou hast much goods laid up for many years; take thine ease, eat, drink, be merry." He was heedless of his comrades of earth, even as he was heedless of God. (*The Parables of Jesus*, page 131)

You see, when we don't include God in our planning, we grow blind to the world around us; we grow blind to other people and their hopes, dreams, needs, and concerns. We also grow blind to God, to God's purposes for our life, and to our spiritual need. So we need to ask, do I include God in my planning about my possessions?

Why Do I Want More?

The third question is a very practical one for those who would escape being possessed by their possessions: Why do I want more? Most of us don't stop to ask that, do we? We get on a roll, as it were, and we don't even question why we are doing what we do every day. Accumulation, gaining more, becomes an end rather than a means.

Why do I want more?

Is it for security? We need to think about that because possessions can give us a false sense of security. Remember that our only real security is in our relationship with God.

Why do I want more? For status and ego identity? Read the parable and notice the language. How clearly it is the language of a self-centered, selfish egotist! Is that the reason we want more? To satisfy our ego, to give us status?

Why do I want more? Is it for the power wealth would give me? How would I use that power? Do I want power over others, or do I want power to share with others in working together for the greater good of all?

What Would I Like to Be Remembered For?

A fourth question to ask ourselves: What would I like to be remembered for?

Shakespeare causes one of his disillusioned agents to cry, "The evil that men do lives after them; the good is often interred with their bones" (*Julius Caesar*, Act 3, Scene 2, Lines 80–81).

History may not be as arbitrary and unprincipled as Shakespeare would suggest, but history does make value-related choices. So we need to ask, what would I like to be remembered for?

> William Allen White gave the city of Emporia a public park of fifty acres as a memorial to his daughter. He directed that it was not to bear his name. When he handed the deed to the mayor, he said: "This is the last kick in a fistful of dollars I am getting rid of today. I have always tried to teach you that there are three kicks in every dollar, one when you make it. . . . The second kick is when you have it. . . . The third kick comes when you give it away. . . . The big kick is the last one." It was a blunt way of saying that the successful, happy life is the giving life. It is also the Christian life. (*Sermons on the Parables of Jesus*, by Charles M. Crowe (Abingdon-Cokesbury Press, 1953); page 127)

Isn't it true that persons are remembered most and best by what they give away—how they spend themselves or refuse to spend themselves in love to others?

When our family gets together—which is becoming rarer now, since they're all grown and building their own lives—do you know what our children talk about? They don't talk about the churches I've served, the honors I've received, the books I've written, my professional achievements. They talk about that tent-trailer we had and our camping trips; about our almost weekly, for a long time, overnight Friday and all day Saturday outings at the beach; about our Thanksgiving celebrations with the McKeithens and the Dickinsons; about our snow vacation between Christmas and New Year. That's what they talk about and that pleases me.

One couple I know of made a life-changing decision about possessions and prestige in order that their children might have memories like these and might also have parents who gave time and energy to the work of the church and to the needs of the community. Both were lawyers. Both ranked high in the esteem of their colleagues and clients. At the time the husband was president of the bar association, they realized that most of their time would be spent advancing in their profession and in making money unless they made a deliberate decision to shape their life in a different way. They decided to set aside time and money for their family and for church and community work. That meant being satisfied with their modest house in an older, but pleasant, part of town, having less expensive cars and fewer "things" than their peers. It meant focusing on others rather than on self.

One could not begin to enumerate the blessings that couple has brought to their church, their community, their family, and their friends. Just as one example, the wife chaired the school board in their city at the time racial integration was mandated by law. She was instrumental in so preparing the community that the transition was made without violence, and for the most part in a spirit of acceptance. But above all else, I expect their children and their friends will remember this couple for the laughter and the pure joy that they brought to all their ventures.

In our daily work, what do we want to be remembered for? George Willis Spann lived in Pueblo, Colorado. They called him "Pop" Spann. For thirty-four years "Pop" was caretaker of the public school in Pueblo.

> He loved and served the children far beyond the call of duty. And they loved him. He listened to their troubles and helped them out of scrapes. He bandaged their hurts and fixed their bicycles. He played with them after school hours even though he had to work later to do his chores. He

strengthened the weaker ones and gave friendship to those who needed it. He loaned them money and bought them presents. He often spent part of his own salary for more equipment for the children. At Christmas he always gave them a paper mural of the Nativity for the cafeteria. All the community came to love and respect this modest, sincere man. Shortly after his retirement, the city of Pueblo built a handsome new school building for $375,000. It proudly bears the name "George Willis Spann" in honor of "Pop," the man who lived a life at the same time he was making a living. (Charles M. Crowe, page 124)

We need to keep on asking, what do I want to be remembered for?

Am I Rich Toward God?

Now the fifth and final question: Am I rich toward God? That's the clinching question, and that's the note on which Jesus closes his parable in verses 20-21: "God said to him, 'Fool! This night your soul is required of you; and the things you have prepared, whose will they be?' So is he who lays up treasures for himself, and is not rich toward God."

What does it mean to be rich toward God? What is true wealth?

In the Dallas-Fort Worth Airport is the mounted skeleton of a plesiosaur. His bones were found during the excavating necessary to build that ultramodern air terminal. The plesiosaur is said to be seventy million years old. He was a great lizard, twenty-five feet long and weighing ten thousand pounds. When you stand in the midst of that monument to the latest in modern technology, you can't help but be impressed by those ancient bones in contrast to this most modern of airports; and the combination of the old and the new—if you're reflective at all—causes you to think about life itself. When centuries have passed, how significant will be the things we allow to cause us anxiety, our wealth, or the other things we presently think are important? The question that has eternal significance is this, "Are we rich toward God?"

What is true wealth?

A clear conscience—cleansed daily by prayer and the forgiving grace of God. That's true wealth—*a clear conscience.*

A committed will—kept strong in a day-by-day Gethsemane: "Not my will, but Thine be done." That's true wealth—*a committed will.*

A caring family—our own husbands, wives, brothers, sisters, parents, children—but also that wider family that is ours when we care and allow others to care out of our love for Christ. That's true wealth—*a loving family.*

A companionship with the living Christ whose love atones for our sins and mistakes, and whose presence is kept alive by our response to the promise of his presence: "Abide in me, and I in you. . . . He who abides in me, and I in him, he it is that bears much fruit, for apart from me you can do nothing" (John 15:4, 5). That's true wealth—*a companionship with the living Christ.*

That's true wealth, and that is the wealth that a certain rich man exchanged for overflowing barns. We don't want to make the same mistake, do we?

For further reflection:

The wording of this parable suggests Psalm 14:
The fool says in his heart,
   "There is no God. . . ."
The Lord looks down from heaven
      upon the children of men,
   to see if there are any that act
wisely,
      that seek after God.

The wording of Luke 12:20, "This night your soul is required of you," carries the connotation that life is a loan given by God. Only a fool forgets that God can require the return of the loan at any time.

> *Experiencing the parable at a deeper level:*
>
> 1. Using whatever method you choose (writing, speaking, round-robin in a group setting, music, artwork, acting, other), express this parable as a modern parable. Use contemporary people, settings, and events that correspond to the first-century examples Jesus used.
> 2. Express the parable using events from your own life that correspond to the events in the parable. What would Jesus say to you?

7. Our Most Common Sin

Pharisee and Tax Collector

Read Luke 18:9-17

What did you think about when you read the chapter title—Our Most Common Sin? What do you think is your most common sin?

Have you heard that old story of the three preachers in the same community, a Baptist, an Episcopalian, and a Methodist, who became rather close? They played golf together and met for coffee. One day they decided that they'd spend two days together just to share and get acquainted, to study a little bit, to talk about their preaching, and to pray.

During the course of that time they evolved in their relationship to the point that they began to confess to one another, to share deeply their inner life.

The Baptist preacher said, "I must confess, fellows, I'm really wrestling with the sin of greed. I never seem to have enough, and I hate to admit it, but for months now I've been taking money out of the collection plate every week. Pray for me."

The Episcopalian priest said, "I understand that kind of uncontrollable urge—my problem is lust. I simply can't keep my eyes off a beautiful woman, and I'm afraid that my lust is going to go beyond just looking."

The Methodist preacher was very quiet, thinking deeply; and the two other fellows looked at him—waiting for him to share his confession. Finally, he broke down. "I'm sorry, guys, my sin is gossip, and I just can't wait to get to a telephone."

Our most common sin—what is it? I believe our most common sin is self-righteousness; or, if you want another label, unhealthy pride. We allow self-righteousness and pride to smother any spark of humility that is within us.

The story of the Pharisee and the tax collector praying in the temple paints a vivid picture of the sin of self-righteous pride and of the redemptive virtue of humility.

We can't miss the meaning of the parable if we notice how it begins. The reason Jesus told the parable is expressed in verse 9: "He also told this parable to some who trusted in themselves that they were righteous and despised others."

The New International Version of the Bible translates the verse this way: "To some who were confident of their own righteousness and looked down on everybody else, Jesus told this parable."

The New English Bible has it, "It was aimed at those who were sure of their own goodness and looked down on everyone else."

The story is simple and straightforward. Two men went up to the temple to pray. One boasted to God of all his good qualities; the other simply asked for God's mercy. The proud man, the Pharisee, was a respected pillar of the church. The humble man was outside the church—almost a religious untouchable. However, he showed his deep humility before God by his attitude in prayer, "he would not even lift up his eyes to heaven." He showed his heartfelt repentance by beating his breast—like women beat their breasts in mourning—as he prayed, "God, be merciful to me a sinner." Jesus said that the favor of God would be upon the untouchable—the one who showed humility—while the judgment of God would be upon the self-righteous one.

I hope we will allow this parable to be a mirror in which we look to see our lives reflected, because I believe we will see in such a mirror the nature and the result of our greatest sin.

The Pitfall of Pride

Let's look briefly at one important facet of the parable of the Pharisee and the tax collector. Note the first part of verse 11: "The Pharisee stood and prayed thus with himself." In that terse word you get the notion that even in prayer the Pharisee was focused on himself.

Listen! Preoccupation with self insinuates the deadly disease of pride into our prayer life and makes our praying ineffective.

The battle between humility and pride is as old as the battle between heaven and hell, and that battle is often fought in our prayer life.

Some of you have read C. S. Lewis' classic little volume, *The Screwtape Letters*. I highly recommend it. In this little volume, Lewis offers thirty-one imaginary letters from Screwtape, a primary personality of the underworld—of hell—to his nephew Wormwood, a junior devil just starting his first assignment on earth, tempting a would-be Christian. The purpose of the correspondence—and it's done very humorously—is to show how hell seeks constantly to divert Christians from following the ways of heaven. In one note, Screwtape tells Wormwood the most productive way to overcome good people is not only to work on their pride, but to infect them with a sense of false pride. Listen to him.

> Catch him at the moment when he is really poor in spirit and smuggle into his mind the gratifying reflection, "By jove! I'm being humble," and almost immediately, pride—pride at his own humility—will appear. If he awakes to the danger, and tries to smother this new form of pride, make him proud of his attempt—and so on, through as many stages as you please. But don't try this too long, for fear you awake his sense of humor and proportion in which case he will merely laugh at you and go to bed. ((The Macmillan Company, 1943); page 63)

Samuel Taylor Coleridge and Robert Southey wrote a poem, "The Devil's Thoughts," that includes the lines,
"And the Devil did grin, for his darling sin
Is pride that apes humility."
The battle between humility and pride is indeed as old as the battle between heaven and hell—and even false pride is a part of the problem. It gets into our praying. When we are preoccupied with self, we are in danger of being infected with the deadly disease of pride, thus our praying becoming ineffective.

Now, being aware of the danger of pride doesn't mean that we must not look at ourselves, that we don't examine our consciences, and confess our sins. That's a very, very important part of praying. To scrutinize our life, to look at ourselves in relation to others, to look at ourselves in relation to God—and to confess our sin and shortcomings is at the heart of prayer.

But Jesus was sounding a different kind of warning. He was sounding a warning against being preoccupied with ourselves. The Pharisee stood and prayed *thus with himself*, and pride prevailed. No one who is proud can pray. "The Gate of Heaven is so low that none can enter it, save upon his knees."

Self-Righteousness Brings Condemnation

Now let's look at the parable in its full impact. The searching light of Jesus' teaching reveals the contrast between self-righteousness and humility—and this parable is clearly a condemnation of self-righteousness and a call to humility. It may be difficult for us to get the full impact of the contrast Jesus is drawing.

> Because we have grown up familiar with the New Testament stories, we have come to accept the Pharisee as a villain. The publican's status is not always clear to us, but we generally assume that he was a fairly decent sort. This was not the feeling of the people who first heard this parable. To them, it was a shocking thing to have a religious teacher speak a good word for the publican and criticize the Pharisee. The publican was regarded as a grafter and a crook. He had sold out his people for a profit and he made his money by oppressing the poor. The Pharisee was learned in the law and punctilious in keeping it. Some listeners no doubt felt like calling out: "Just a minute, Teacher. Did you mean what you have just said? Did you not get the characters reversed?"
>
> If a modern preacher should tell a story with a gangster as the hero and a priest as the rascal, the congregation might wonder at his sanity. To say the least, should a gangster ever be portrayed in a favorable light? It is bad enough when he gets his just deserts. Or is it wise, we might ask, ever to picture a minister in an unfavorable light? After all, even Hollywood has a code regarding such matters. So we may appreciate something of the dramatic effect of the parable on the people who first heard it. (*The Parables*, by Gerald Kennedy (Harper & Brothers, 1960); pages 116–117)

But that is really the contrast Jesus is drawing—dramatic as it may be.

"A medieval monk said that everyone who gets to heaven will be surprised by three things. First, he will be surprised to see many he did not think would be there. Second, he will be surprised that some are not there whom he expected to see. Third, he will be surprised that he himself is there" (Gerald Kennedy, pages 118–119).

Certainly we have a surprise here in this parable. The most outcast of persons, as far as religion is concerned, is accepted; the most likely candidate for heaven, as far as religion is concerned, is condemned. And all because of our most common sin—self-righteousness. So, let's focus on that core problem—self-righteousness.

Self-righteousness is goodness gone to seed. Are you familiar with the farm image—gone to seed? When we say that a plant has gone to seed, we mean that the fruit or vegetable that was to be produced has been jumped over—and only seed is there.

Again, let's look at the Pharisee. He would not be judged a bad man in any community or group in which he might find himself in society today. In his own day, he was a member of the Jewish group that represented the highest in ethics and religion, the group that most conscientiously tried to keep the law and to encourage all others to do so as well. Pharisees were the recognized leaders and representatives of Jewish religious faith and practice. This Pharisee's friends might have regarded him as a bit pompous and critical, not their favorite dinner guest, but they would have accepted him as a virtuous man.

His prayer was no doubt perfectly true on the surface. He was, in truth, not an extortioner, nor an adulterer, nor unjust; moreover, he *was*, as he said, faithful in his religious duties; he fasted twice a week and gave a tenth of his income to the synagogue. All these practices were more than the law required. However, this Pharisee had not taken to heart the message of the prophets:

> For thus says the high and lofty One
>   who inhabits eternity, whose
>   name is Holy:
> "I dwell in the high and holy place,
>   and also with him who is of a
>   contrite and humble spirit. . . ."
> (Isaiah 57:15)

He has showed you, O man, what is good;
and what does the Lord require of you
but to do justice, and to love kindness,
and to walk humbly with your God?
(Micah 6:8)

This Pharisee is a perfect example of what Paul described in 1 Corinthians 13. Without love, all his virtues amounted to nothing. His self-proclaimed goodness was barren. It had gone to seed; it bore no fruit.

On the other hand, Jesus declared that the tax collector, who was held in contempt by his fellow citizens as an extortioner and as an agent of his nation's conquerors, went down to his house justified. "Jesus was saying here, in no uncertain terms, that pride can cancel out our virtues and that humility can overcome many a sin in the sight of God" (*Sermons on the Parables of Jesus,* by Charles M. Crowe (Abingdon Press, 1953); page 167).

At the heart of Jesus' teaching is a warning against a religion that becomes a mechanical matter of routine observance or habit.

When our religion becomes a mechanical matter of routine observances, it will go stagnant and flat, and there are a lot of stagnant and flat Christians around. We may keep all the rules and perform all the duties. But if we're not humble in spirit—if were not teachable in mind—if we're not understanding of soul—we will lose the way.

Self-Righteousness Separates Us From Our Best Selves

An insidious characteristic of self-righteousness is that it tends to compare our best with others' worst. (That same tendency in making comparisons is also true of nations.) Therefore, the self-righteous are always the self-satisfied. The Pharisee was pleased to compare himself with one whom society regarded as the lowest. "Measured by other men, he towered aloft. It had not occurred to him to measure himself by the sky" (*The Parables of Jesus,* by George A. Buttrick (Baker, 1973); page 88). Self-satisfaction is the enemy of growth.

Another danger of self-righteousness is that it may make us more interested in appearances than in solid accomplishments.

There is a story about a mountaineer who established a great reputation for himself as a marksman. Whoever followed him around found target rings on trees and fences with a bullet hole in the center. Asked to explain the secret of his skill, he answered, "It is easy. I just shoot and draw a circle around the hole."

This is the method of the Pharisee. We present our accomplishments to the world as superior by making them appear the result of superior virtue. But the Greek word for sin is "*hamartia*" and it means "to miss the mark." When we aim at the target honestly we do not hit many bull's eyes. On the contrary, we have to confess poor marksmanship and many failures. (Kennedy, page 123)

Jesus is telling us that only those who are humble enough to admit that they have missed the mark are going to be accepted. Only those who are humble enough to admit they have missed the target have hope of improving their marksmanship.

When we are self-righteous, we have no sense of the possibilities open before us because we have no sense of our need to grow. We have no gracious ability to acknowledge to others—or to God—our sins and shortcomings; therefore, we spend a great deal of energy on self-justification. We take no delight in the accomplishments of others, and, therefore, we do not learn from others. We do not go through the doors to new worlds that others may open for us. We have no sense of our need for God's forgiveness and God's grace; therefore, we never experience the new life God offers us in Jesus Christ.

As Christians, we have a sure cure for self-righteousness. When we measure ourselves against Jesus, we fall so far short that we have no room for any self-righteousness at all. Yet we have the assurance of the writer of the Epistle to the Hebrews that

. . . we have not a high priest who is unable to sympathize with our weaknesses, but one who in every respect has been tempted as we are, yet without sin. Let us then with confidence draw near to the throne of grace, that we may receive mercy and find grace to help in time of need. (4:15-16)

But how tragic it would be if we let self-righteousness come between us and that grace or between us and the promise in the First Epistle of John: "Beloved, we are God's children now; it does not yet appear what we shall be, but we know that when he appears we shall be like him . . ." (3:2).

Self-Righteousness Separates Us From Others

A third warning about self-righteousness is that it separates us from our brothers and sisters in the human family.

There is a story of the Sunday school teacher who, after telling this story of the Pharisee and the tax collector, said, "Now children, let us thank God that we're not like the nasty Pharisee." You see, she was guilty of the same sin as the Pharisee, who said, "Thank God, I'm not as that tax collector." Self-righteousness separates us from our brothers and sisters in the human family. It separates us from others because it causes us to seek to establish worth and judgment on the basis of comparison. We determine our worth and/or the worth of another by comparing them to us and us to them.

When we look at ourselves honestly in the mirror of this parable, most of us will see some vestiges of the Pharisee within us. We may pride ourselves on our intelligence, our education, our cultural achievements, our wealth, our social position, our race, our religion, our nationality, our political position, our morality, even on our ability to be on time. Nothing is too insignificant to be cause for self-congratulation at the expense of others.

One of my favorite stories is about two college freshmen in an Ivy League university who, after the first semester's grades were posted, spotted each other as chief rivals for valedictorian. They did not meet each other, but they read their names, one above the other, on the bulletin board. Each, on his own, decided on a strategy that would assure his victory at the end of four years.

Each semester, as the grades were posted outside their professors' doors, they carefully monitored their progress toward their goal. And each semester, one of them would be on the top, the other barely below. First one on the top and then the other. All those who were interested in grades were acutely aware of the competition.

Now, though they recognized each other, they never met. Neither of them ever made a gesture of friendship. When the time came for graduation, sure enough, one of the made valedictorian and the other salutatorian. Each walked across the stage and received his diploma, and each disappeared to take up his chosen profession.

Forty years later, one of them was a portly and balding gentleman, dressed in the elaborate robes of the church and the red beanie that signified that he was a cardinal—this portly and balding gentleman, dressed in his linen and satin and rich colors, entered Grand Central Station. Immediately he spotted his collegiate rival—the man with whom he had competed throughout college. He was tall and ramrod straight—dressed in a snappy military uniform with four stars across his shoulders—a general.

The portly gentleman with his red beanie thought, *Here we are, former college mates and leaders of our respective professions, and we've never even met one another. The least I could do as a man of the cloth is to take the initiative and speak to my rival.* So he crossed the busy Grand Central reception room, faced his collegiate arch rival and said, "Conductor, can you tell me when the next train leaves for Chicago?"

The four-star General responded, "I don't know, *Madam*; but should a woman in your condition be traveling?"

Self-righteousness leads us to establish worth and judgment on the basis of comparison and competition. It does not take into account the obstacles others may have faced and overcome. It does not take into account our indebtedness to others for all that we have and are, and thus it separates us from our brothers and sisters in the human family.

Pride and self-righteousness can not live with the law of the kingdom of God that we love our neighbor as we love ourselves. In God's kingdom our whole attitude toward others is one of rejoicing in their successes, of appreciation for their worth, and of gratitude for all we receive from their hands.

Self-Righteousness Separates Us From God

But not only does self-righteousness separate us from our fellow human beings, causing us to want to establish worth and judgment on the basis of competition and comparison; it separates us from God. And that's the ultimate warning of this parable. Self-righteousness separates us from God.

Experiencing the parable at a deeper level:

1. Using whatever method you choose (writing, speaking, round-robin in a group setting, music, artwork, acting, other), express this parable as a modern parable. Use contemporary people, settings, and events that correspond to the first-century examples Jesus used.
2. Express the parable using events from your own life that correspond to the events in the parable. What would Jesus say to you?

8. Practicing Humility

Places at the Table

Read Luke 14:7-11

Jesus told another parable, recorded in Luke 14:7-11, about humility and pride and self-righteousness. One sabbath when he was invited to dinner at the home of a Pharisee, Jesus observed how the guests contended with one another for the seats of honor at the table. At dinner he told them a parable about taking seats at a wedding banquet. Jesus said that when you are invited to a wedding feast, don't sit at the place of honor. It may be that some more important person than you has been invited. Though your host has invited you both, he might have to come to you and say, "Give place to this man." If that happened, then you would have to take the lower place in shame. Save yourself from that—he said. Go and sit in the lowest place so that when the host comes, he can invite you to come up higher. That will bring honor to you rather than shame.

Jesus was not giving a lesson in etiquette. He was teaching about the kingdom of God, and the Pharisees could not miss the point. He was telling them in the plainest way possible that there was no place for their pride in status or their assumption of honor in the kingdom of God. In God's kingdom, God, the host, is going to seat people as he thinks they deserve, and the humble person is going to fare far better than the proud one. Jesus closed that parable with this word: "For everyone who exalts himself will be humbled, and he who humbles himself will be exalted."

Self-righteousness separates us from God because the self-righteous feel no need for God. Jesus said of the self-righteous, "They have their reward." They have what they are looking for; they don't know that they need anything from God.

Humility Gives Hope

In this verse from the "Shepherd Boy's Song," John Bunyan presents a contrast to those who are always expecting places of honor:
He that is down needs fear no fall,
  He that is low no pride.
  He that is humble ever shall
  Have God to be his guide.
Those who are humble can rest in the hope that they will not seek God's guidance in vain.

The story of Jesus and the children follows the parable of the Pharisee and the tax collector. Children had no status and little importance in Jesus' day, but Jesus said, "Let the children come to me." He continued to emphasize the lesson of the parable of the Pharisee and the tax collector with these words, "Truly, I say to you, whoever does not receive the kingdom of God like a child shall not enter it." Children know their need. They are open to love, and they are eager to grow. The Kingdom belongs to those who have the openness and humility of children. Pride shuts the door on growth and new life. Humility opens the way to possibilities that only the grace of God can fathom. Paul wrote:

Not that I have already obtained this [the resurrection from the dead] or am already perfect; but I press on to make it my own, because Christ Jesus has made me his own. Brethren, I do not consider that I have made it my own; but one thing I do, forgetting what lies behind and straining forward to what lies ahead, I press on toward the goal for the prize of the upward call of God in Christ Jesus. (Philippians 3:12-14)

For the humble, for those who know they have not yet attained the prize, there is always the hope of something more.

The story is told that when the Emperor of Austria-Hungary died during World War I, after ruling for more than sixty years, he was carried as his forebears before him to the crypt of the Church of the Capuchins in Vienna. When the escort knocked at the gate, a voice from inside offered the traditional challenge, "Who is there?" The reply came, "His supreme Majesty, the Emperor of Austria." The grave-side liturgist responded, "I know him not. Who is there?" Again, the answer, "the apostolic king of Hungary." Once more the voice inside responded, "I know him not. Who is there?" The escort this time declared: "Our brother, Frans-Joseph, a sinner."

At those words, the gates opened.

And so it always is—not the self-righteous, not those who are always going around putting the circle around the shot they've made trying to prove that it was a bull's eye—but those who know that they've missed the mark, those who know that they're sinners, those who are willing to confess their sins, and seek mercy—it's those for whom the gates are opened, who go away from God's presence justified.

For further reflection:

The parable of the places at the table recalls Proverbs 25:6-7:
Do not put yourself forward in the
   king's presence
   or stand in the place of the great;
for it is better to be told, "Come up
    here,"
   than to be put lower in the
presence of the prince.

As in our day, the most honored guests often arrived last; therefore, to take the place of honor would invite the probability of being asked to move.

Experiencing the parable at a deeper level:

1. Using whatever method you choose (writing, speaking, round-robin in a group setting, music, artwork, acting, other), express this parable as a modern parable. Use contemporary people, settings, and events that correspond to the first-century examples Jesus used.
2. Express the parable using events from your own life that correspond to the events in the parable. What would Jesus say to you?

9. How Do We Get Rid of Evil Without Destroying Good?

Wheat and Tares

Read Matthew 13:24-30

How do we deal with evil? More precisely, how do we get rid of evil without destroying good?

The parable of the wheat and tares addresses the question. Like all of our Lord's parables, this one comes straight from the life of his own day, from the experiences and observations of the people who listened so eagerly to his teaching. However, we in our day find this parable a bit hard to understand because this incident could not have occurred in the wheat-growing sections of America. We know about farms stretching over hundreds and hundreds and hundreds of acres. The sowing and the reaping is done by sophisticated farm machinery. Land is sprayed before it is planted in order to minimize the possibility of weeds. Then if weeds grow after the crop comes up, they will be dealt with by spraying weed-killing chemicals, not by uprooting the plants.

So, we have to shift gears in our mind. Jesus is talking about a small country—Palestine—where farm land was scarce and individual tracts were small, where sowing and reaping were done by hand. So, get the story clearly in mind.

A man sowed his field with good grain and then went to sleep. As he slept, an enemy sprinkled the field with a seed that produced a weed which, in its early stages, looked so much like wheat that the two could hardly be told apart. As the wheat and the weeds grew, discerning servants recognized that something was wrong and brought word of the problem to the farmer. After a survey of his crop, he agreed with them that an enemy had tried to ruin him—had come in and sowed weed seed in his wheat. What should he do? What could he do? Go over the field inch-by-inch and pull out the weeds? That was a possibility, but in all probability it would be impossible to pull out the weeds without ruining the good grain. The master concluded that there was only one thing to do: "Let both grow together until the harvest; and at the harvest time I will tell the reapers, 'Gather the weeds first and bind them in bundles to be burned, but gather the wheat into my barn' " (Matthew 13:30).

Let me tell another story, a contemporary one, that might help us get into this parable. Harold Bosley shared this incident that occurred while he was in Harrisburg, Pennsylvania. He was at the old capitol building in that city, now a museum, studying again the huge painting of Pickett's charge at the Battle of Gettysburg during the Civil War. As he stood gazing at the painting, he noticed in front of him a mother and two small sons who were seated, looking at the picture.

The older boy asked, "Which are the good guys and which are the bad guys in that picture?"

His mother replied softly, "It's hard to tell."

"Why are they trying to kill each other?" the boy persisted. The mother answered slowly, telling about slavery and other troubles.

"Did they have to fight?" the boy asked.

The mother's reply showed the mark of wisdom: "They thought so."

> There was in that reply the gentleness distilled in the interval of a hundred years. Gone the sharpness, the harshness of snap judgments—now, an awareness not only of the evil of slavery but also of the equally great evil of what can only be called the will to misunderstand, to misrepresent, and to misjudge people who disagree with us. (*He Spoke to Them in Parables*, by Harold A. Bosley (Harper & Row Publishers, 1963); page 127)

Do we need evidence to confirm the adage: Two wrongs do not make a right? Certainly the tragic chapter of the Civil War and the period of slavery in the experience of our country is ample evidence. But I tell the story to make the parable clear. It is not always easy to discern what is evil and what is good. But more particularly, it is almost never easy to discern who is evil and who is good. Evil and goodness are often a strange mixture. Attacking evil sometimes does more harm to good than it does to evil—that is, the weapons we use in our fight against evil, the attitudes that pervade, what happens to us as we engage ourselves in the battle, the estrangement that takes place, the misunderstandings—the way we attack one evil sometimes creates a second evil as bad as the first. So, let's try to deal with the parable and keep the question in the back of our minds, "How do we get rid of evil without destroying good?"

An Enemy Is at Work

Let's begin with a sobering fact that must not be ignored: There is "an enemy" operating against us in our world.

Now, I don't believe this fact is the primary reason Jesus told the parable, but it's such a part of the parable that we cannot ignore it. More important, it's such a fact of life that we dare not close our eyes to it. "An enemy" is operating against us in our world.

There was, in Jesus' day, a well-known weed, a poisonous, bearded darnel that looked so much like wheat that the rabbis called it "a perverted kind of wheat." Jesus' audience knew about that weed and understood how easy it was for an enemy to destroy a crop by sowing the seed of this perverted kind of wheat in the real wheat. That image is suggestive for us as we think about the enemy that works against us. Oftentimes that enemy is not recognized. Many times the enemy is a perverted kind of goodness—at least it masquerades as goodness.

So, let's begin with the recognition that Jesus does not blink at the grim fact of the presence of evil in the world. Here in this parable, as he did again and again, he brings us face to face with the horrid and ugly fact of sin and evil.

> Whatever explanation we give of the presence of sin does not in the slightest degree change its reality. However we undertake to explain it, there is one thing that we certainly cannot do, and that is explain it away. Look where we will, there are tares growing among the wheat. There is good being elbowed by evil. There is wrong dwelling in the closest proximity with right.

We recognize this fact as we look at humanity as a whole. We're sure that God did not fling this world from his fingers to let it shift for itself. Jesus taught emphatically that this is God's world, and that God is forever interested and active in it. But in spite of the presence of God, in spite of the activities of all the saints, in spite of the struggles of the missionaries, in spite of the death of the martyrs, in spite of all the heroisms of all the centuries in the cause of righteousness, sin has not been driven out of one single nation. It has not been driven out of one single city. It has not been driven out of one single hamlet. It has not even been completely and perfectly exterminated in one single home in the world. Go where you will, in Christendom or outside it, and you will find tares growing among wheat. (*Sermons from the Parables*, by Clovis G. Chappell (Abingdon Press, 1933); page 38)

Therefore, in the beginning we need to register this grim truth: the fact of an enemy operating against us in our world. Good and evil are real facts to be encountered and dealt with. Also, good and evil are as different as weeds and wheat. At times there may be tentative confusion about which is which, but ultimately the distinction is made, must be made, will be made.

We Must Live With Imperfection

Now, let's move to a second truth, a second truth that really strikes at the heart of our daily life. While we are involved in a search for perfection, we must live with imperfection. Gerald Kennedy reminds us that in this parable "the field is a man's life, and he must come to terms immediately with the uncomfortable truth that it will always have weeds in it. Why this is so has been the theme of many philosophies, but all we need to know is that a field of mixed wheat and weeds is a good picture of life" (*The Parables* (Harper & Brothers 1960); pages 46–47).

Some time ago, in an annual charity baseball game between the comedians and the actors, Groucho Marx was made manager of the comedians. He had Jack Benny lead off and said to him, "All right, Benny, get up there and hit a home run." Benny struck out, whereupon Marx resigned, saying, "I can't manage a team that won't follow instructions" (Kennedy, page 48).

100

That's worth a chuckle, but when you think of it as a bizarre act on Groucho's part—which it was—it really is no more unreasonable than some of our reactions to life. We demand the impossible, and we resign when the best is denied us.

While we are involved in a search for perfection, we must live with imperfection.

One common point of reference should convince us of the fact that we must live with imperfection—home and family relationships. Marriages may be made in heaven, but marriage partners are fallible, sinful, less-than-perfect human beings. Husband and wife may not always think first of the other's needs and wishes, may not take into account the other's disappointments and frustrations with work, with personal goals, and with family relationships. It is certain that neither partner will be a perfect parent, nor will the children be paragons of perfection. Most husbands and wives will, at times, be irritating, maddening, and downright infuriating. Yet seeking another husband or wife is no solution to the problem. His or her faults will be just as numerous and perhaps more intolerable than those of our present marriage partner. We must learn to live with imperfections in ourselves and in those we love.

Now that's the big point—and we can apply it to the whole of life—we must learn to live with imperfections in our ourselves, in our colleagues, and in those we love.

Our life in the church must be lived out against the backdrop of this truth. In fact, "the early church treasured this parable and used it steadily as they tried to deal with the conflict between evil doers in their fellowship and the purists who wanted to throw them out" (Bosley, page 125).

Some scholars believe that Jesus told this parable in the context of debating the question of what to do with Judas Iscariot, who was already showing signs of defection. Should Jesus send him packing? If he did, what would be the effect of this dismissal on the ones who remained? "Perhaps we ought to let him stay until we are sure he is no longer one of us," he reasoned. "Then it will be time enough to tell him to leave the group" (Bosley, page 125).

Whether this conjecture was the actual case or not, it could have been so because the mark of Jesus' ministry was patient love and care—giving everyone the benefit of the doubt. Paul took the same position of patience that Jesus did. "Evil doers are to be warned, prayed over, given every chance to mend their ways, and only as a last resort, asked to leave the fellowship" (Bosley, page 125).

You remember that specific word in Galatians 6:1-2: "Brethren, if a man is overtaken in any trespass, you who are spiritual should restore him in a spirit of gentleness. Look to yourself, lest you too be tempted. Bear one another's burdens, and so fulfil the law of Christ."

Two notions about the church are always in conflict. One notion is that the church is a "called-out people"—called out from the world to be pure in every way—pure in morality and pure in doctrine, untainted by the world. In some cases, the emphasis is upon doctrine; and in other instances, on morality. I heard one of the most popular television preachers expound on this idea one Sunday afternoon not long ago. He was urging people to leave churches where the preacher was not proclaiming the pure, unadulterated doctrine of Scripture. Of course, he was the one—and those who believed as he did—who determined what pure doctrine was.

One wonders how people like that can stay sane, certainly how they can live with what is a blatantly arrogant position. What do they say God is going to do with the entire Methodist Church, or the Presbyterian, or the Episcopal, or the Lutheran, or the Catholic Church? Doctrine is important; but let's never forget Jesus' biggest confrontation was with the Pharisees, purists in doctrine—those who made right belief and right interpretation of law the ultimate route to God.

According to my observation, some of the groups that are rigid in doctrine and purists in their belief are also cold and calloused in their treatment of others—to my mind, furthest from the compassionate mind of Christ.

Others who hold to the notion that the church is to be "called out people—untainted by the world," put their emphasis on morality. And usually the emphasis is upon what they would call "sins of the flesh." They refuse to marry people who have been divorced. They excommunicate people who they think are not living up to their standards.

That's one notion of the church—"A called-out people, pure in doctrine and morality, untainted by the world."

The other notion, in conflict with this one, sees the church, not as "a refuge for saints, but as a hospital for sinners." Now that may be putting it too simply, but you get the point. This understanding of the church puts the emphasis on the continuing grace of God and on the growth of persons. The emphasis is upon the ongoing nature of salvation and the Lordship of Christ. We recognize that there is so much good in the worst of us, and so much bad in the best of us, that only the grace of a loving God can save any one of us, that judgment belongs to God and not to us.

It's obvious that mine is the latter understanding of the church. But don't distort the understanding. The church is a called-out people—and our call is to holiness and righteousness and justice. I agree with the Chief Executive of the Assemblies of God in his response to the Jimmy-Tammy Bakker situation. The Rev. G. Raymond Carlson said, among other things, "the church is a shining light in the darkness of a crooked and perverse generation and stands as a bulwark against the onslaughts of immoral filth which seeks to engulf our world" (*The United Methodist Reporter*, August 21, 1987, page 2).

I agree with that. The church and Christians are to serve as "a spiritual and moral beacon amid a fallen world."

Even so, we don't sacrifice our ministry of love and redemption in order to have a body of true believers pure in doctrine and impeccable in moral performance. We don't destroy the wheat that is trying to grow by pulling up by the tares that may have slipped into the field, or even that may have been planted there by the enemy.

Shall We Pull Up The Tares?

Now the third truth—the main issue of the parable: How do we get rid of evil without destroying good?

The servants and the master both were committed to getting rid of evil. The conflict is in the method. Jesus is committed to that—to ridding our hearts and the world of evil. We servants of Jesus must likewise be committed to getting rid of evil. But we must be careful about the method.

The servants in the parable wanted to pull up the renegade tares. In their suggestion they set a pattern that has persisted until now.

Tare-pulling is one of the most appealing methods of dealing with evil that our world has ever known. In spite of the fact that Jesus did not sanction this method, his servants have never been able to let it alone. There's something tremendously appealing about the pulling of tares. If

103

an evil is present, destroy it. If there is a false doctrine, demolish it. If there is a pagan idol, smash it. If there is a temple built to idolatry, tear it down. If there are tares growing among the wheat, pay no attention to the wheat, look to the tares and pull them up.

But while this method of dealing with evil is very appealing and while the man who employs it will always have a following, it has certain obvious defects. It is easy for us to see why Jesus did not give it his sanction. First, it requires a wisdom, a power of judgment, that we do not possess. It looks as if anyone could tell wheat from tares, or tares from wheat, but such is not the case. . . . Good and evil depend upon that something called motive . . . therefore, we are not to spend our time pulling tares because to do so requires on our part a wisdom that belongs to God alone.

In the second place, such a procedure endangers the wheat. Assuming that the puller of tares is himself wheat, it endangers him. No man, however good he may be at the beginning, can set himself up as the judge of his brother without desperate hurt to his own soul. . . . The church or the individual that sets out in such critical manner to compel others to conform to their standards in every particular will gravitate toward hardness and harshness and unbrotherliness as naturally as night follows day.

Then tare-pulling endangers the wheat that grows beside it. We used to turn unworthy members out of the church. There are those today who lament the fact that this is no longer done. Far be it from me to argue for laxness. Yet I have some members in my own church that, so far as I am able to judge, are very unworthy. One of these is a husband and father. Suppose I pull up this ugly tare and fling him out of the field. It would possibly be no better than he deserves, but I hesitate for these reasons: If love will not win him to a good life, ostracism will not. Then his life is interlocked with that of a good woman who is his wife. In addition he has some lovely children. These also would be hurt.

. . . The tares and the wheat are so interlocked that it is hard to pull up one without injury to the other. (Chappell, pages 41–44)

When I was a boy growing up in rural Mississippi, I used to chop cotton and hoe corn. I would often find a weed growing very close to a stalk of corn or cotton. I would undertake to cut this weed, but in the process, how many times have I cut the corn and cotton also.

During World War II, our supply of quinine was diminished at a time when many of our men were fighting in malaria-infested areas of the world. A team of scientists went to the Atlanta Federal Prison and asked for volunteers to help find a new cure for malaria. Three hundred men responded and risked their lives by being infected with malaria. As a result of their suffering, chloroquine was developed and saved many lives.

When each volunteer was given an emblem to wear on his sleeve, one man refused, saying, "I don't want any credit—this is the only decent thing I ever did."

It's not always easy to discern what is evil and what is good. All of us are a strange mixture of wheat and tares. Attacking evil sometimes does more harm to good than to evil. So remember—stay close to the Lord of the harvest! Let the Lord call the shots and make the judgments.

So how do we get rid of evil without destroying good? The Master said, "Let both grow together until the harvest." We can take it that, in this, Jesus is suggesting for us a remedy, a style of dealing with evil. Two things seem to be clear. First, Jesus, is counseling *patience*. He's counseling patience, but let's be clear.

Patience is not softness due to lack of conviction; patience is firmness born of conviction and sustained by a purpose guided by a gentleness which knows that time and persistence are essentials of all enduring victories.

The question, "Shall we be patient with evil?" admits of only one answer when held in the light of the Christian ethic: "Yes—as patient as God is with sinners like us and the evil in our lives."

What a different kind of home, church, community, and world we would have if the human point of this parable could get through to our calloused consciences and hard hearts. No more snap judgments! No more hurrying from headline to headline in frantic haste! No more execution of character by hearsay and gossip when someone disagrees with us even in fundamental matters! None of these, but a willingness to let both grow together to the harvest and the infinite patience to let the truth be proved by the event itself. . . .

Here, as elsewhere, Jesus shows us the way.

He heard the word, "sinner" applied freely to persons round about him. And it was more than a word then. It had real bite to it. It indicated someone you could not associate with or exchange greetings with, even though you knew him by name. You would deny every form of deep fellowship with him. To call a person a sinner was to make him an outcast—and you were supposed to separate yourself voluntarily from all relationships with him. It is a striking thing that our Lord paid little or no attention to the distinctions that were supposed to separate sinners and saints. He knew that there was much more to a person than any sin he might have committed. He was a child of God, a person who needed God, a creature in search of his Creator, a child in need of his Father, and—lest we forget—a human being in need of a friend. Jesus took the time, in loving patience, to know the sinner in this deeper dimension of his being—his spirit and soul—and he loved him all the more because of his need. (Bosley, pages 131–132)

I ask you, where would you be if someone had not been patient with you?

Put Your Emphasis On The Wheat

The second thing Jesus teaches us in the parable is this: Put your emphasis on the wheat, not the tares. His was a positive gospel—a gospel that recognized the tares in the field of our life, but cultivated the wheat as the saving answer. Listen to him:

"And as you wish that men would do to you, do so to them. If you love those who love you, what credit is that to you? For even sinners love those who love them. . . . But love your enemies, and do good, . . . and your reward will be great. . . . Be merciful, even as your Father is merciful. Judge not, and you will not be judged; condemn not, and you will not be condemned; forgive, and you will be forgiven; give, and it will be given to you; good measure, pressed down, shaken together, running over, will be put in your lap. For the measure you give will be the measure you get back" (Luke 6:31-32, 35-39). "A new commandment I give unto you that ye love one another; even as I have loved you" (John 13:34).

Paul preached the same strategy: "Be not overcome of evil, but overcome evil with good." The only remedy that can be effectively used against evil is the opposite—goodness. Paul knew many Gentile converts who were finding the Christian life difficult. Pagan customs were an integral part of their lives. How did Paul tell them to go about changing their lives? He did not order them to clench their fists and square their jaws and vow that they would never touch the unclean thing again. He did not counsel them to pull up the tares that were growing in their hearts one by one; nor did he preach in such a way as to encourage us to brood over our follies and defects. But this is his direction, and it is open to the weak and the strong, to the young and the old.

One, be patient. Two, replace sin and evil in your own life with goodness—and use goodness as your antidote for sin and evil in others and in the world. Jesus' method won for others; it will win for you and me. "This I say, walk in the Spirit, and ye shall not fulfill the lust of the flesh" (Galatians 5:19, KJV).

So how do we get rid of evil without destroying good?

"Leave it alone until the harvest," that's what Jesus said, God's ways may seem slow, but they are powerful and sure. God's timetable is based on a wise and patient law of growth—"until the harvest!" A favorite Thanksgiving hymn based on the parable of the wheat and tares recognizes this truth.

All the world is God's own field,
Fruit unto his praise to yield;
Wheat and tares together sown,
Unto joy or sorrow grown;
First the blade, and then the ear,
Then the full corn shall appear;
Lord of harvest, grant that we
Wholesome grain and pure may be.

For the Lord our God shall come,
And shall take his harvest home;
From his field shall in that day
All offenses purge away,
Give his angels charge at last

In the fire the tares to cast,
But the fruitful ears to store
In his garner evermore.

—Henry Alford

Now, we can't ignore a final suggestion in this parable. Life has its end-time, its climax, its judgment. As James Russell Lowell wrote about it: "Some great cause, God's new Messiah, offering each the bloom or blight, parts the goats upon the left hand and the sheep upon the right" ("The Present Crisis").

"Leave it alone until the harvest," the Master said. God will judge and will give instructions for the harvest: "Gather up first the tares and bind them in bundles to burn them, but gather the wheat into the barn." We don't have to rush the judgment nor do we take it into our own hands. Let harvest time come and trust the Lord.

Rehearse now what we have said the parable teaches us:

One, *there is an enemy operating against us in our world.*

Two, *while we seek perfection, we must learn to live with imperfection.*

Three, in trying to get rid of sin and evil without destroying good, *we must practice patience. We must put our emphasis on the wheat, not the tares, and leave judgment to God.* Then we will be able to sing confidently the last stanza of that Thanksgiving hymn:

Even so, Lord, quickly come,
Bring thy final harvest home;
Gather thou thy people in,
Free from sorrow, free from sin,
There, forever purified,
In thy presence to abide;
Come, with all thine angels, come,
Raise the glorious harvest home.

For further reflection:

Jesus lived at a time when many groups were trying to set up the pure community that followed God's commands in every particular, kept the law perfectly, and devoted themselves exclusively to faithful religious practice. The Pharisees were one such group within society. John the Baptist called people into the wilderness to repent. The Essenes and the people of the Dead Sea Scrolls—who were probably one and the same—lived in communities apart in order to be pure. Against this background Jesus told the parable of the wheat and the tares.

Experiencing the parable at a deeper level:

1. Using whatever method you choose (writing, speaking, round-robin in a group setting, music, artwork, acting, other), express this parable as a modern parable. Use contemporary people, settings, and events that correspond to the first-century examples Jesus used.
2. Express the parable using events from your own life that correspond to the events in the parable. What would Jesus say to you?

---

10. WHAT TO DO WHEN YOU HAVE BEEN FORGIVEN

The Unforgiving Servant

Read Matthew 18:21-35

The parable of the unforgiving servant would make a thrilling action-packed drama. Our minds are riveted on the rapidly changing scene and setting. It begins in the luxury of a king's palace, moves to a bustling street in a busy, Eastern city, with the sounds and sights and smells of the trading stalls—then on to the dark, damp dungeon of a primitive prison—then back again into the rich luxury of the king's palace.

The drama unfolds rapidly, keeping us attentively on the edge of our mental seats. Our feelings are stirred and change rapidly. We feel sympathy for the man who owed such a staggering debt. The king angers us at once because he's going to exact every ounce of life from his debtor. Then abruptly the king is no longer a villain, but a hero in his compassion, and we are flabbergasted at the extent of his mercy. Our anger rises to its highest pitch as the now-forgiven debtor lays hands on a man who owes just a pittance and throws him into jail. We breathe a sigh of satisfaction, maybe self-righteous satisfaction, when the king brings the unforgiving debtor back to judgment and delivers him to be tormented until his huge, un-payable debt is satisfied.

If this parable were staged or filmed, it would be worth at least a Thursday-night-at-the-movies on television. It would probably make a hit in a Broadway theater. The problem we must overcome is a tendency to see the parable in that fashion—as a drama—with us as spectators. That way of looking at the parable won't help us—beyond providing some entertainment—and we dare not take it so lightly. Jesus saw this drama as one in which we are all participants. He told the story in response to Peter's question, "Lord, how often shall my brother sin against me, and I forgive him? As many as seven times?"

Jesus answered him, "I do not say to you seven times, but seventy times seven!" But that wasn't enough for Jesus. He went on to tell the parable of the unforgiving servant to make clear what forgiveness is like in the kingdom of heaven.

So Jesus is calling us with this parable, calling us to get on the stage ourselves, to recognize that this drama is our life, because nothing is more at the center of life than forgiveness, than forgiving and being forgiven.

In a twentieth-century drama that most of us know better than we know this parable, the tension surrounding forgiveness is set to music. You remember the musical, *My Fair Lady*. Professor Henry Higgins gets caught in the all-too-human ambivalence toward forgiveness. Eliza Doolittle is tearing him apart. In his frustration over her, he hears himself claiming to be a forgiving sort of person; nevertheless he finds it almost impossible to forgive her. He sings, "I am a most forgiving man."

Like most of us, however, he can't stick to that understanding of himself with consistency. His temper gets the better of him and he adds another set of lyrics:

> But I will never take her back,
> if she were crawling on her knees!
> Let her promise to atone,
> let her shiver, let her moan.
> I will slam the door
> and let the hell cat freeze!

We know the tension, don't we? The tension between applauding forgiveness in general, but refusing to offer forgiveness in the specific. Yes, Jesus is setting forth our own dramas in this parable. When we read it subjectively, it leaves us with some anxious questions and concerns, and that's what Jesus wanted. Therefore, as far as possible, let's look at the parable from the inside.

The parable as one big point: God's forgiveness of us is dependent upon our forgiveness of others. We'll come back to that central message, but the parable also suggests some other truths that we must not ignore.

There Will Always Be a Day of Reckoning

First, there will always be a day of reckoning.

Note verse 23: "Therefore the kingdom of heaven may be compared to a king who wishes to settle accounts with his servants." Another translation (RV) uses the word *reckoning*. "Therefore is the kingdom of heaven likened unto a certain king, *which would make a reckoning with his servants.*"

Mark this down in your mind. "A citizen of the kingdom of God is one who has made a full reckoning with God over the question of sin and guilt" (*Many Things in Parables*, by Ronald S. Wallace (Harper & Brothers, 1955); page 170).

In this parable, then, we have a picture of God seeking to reckon with us— each one of us personally—about the matter of our sin and guilt.

> In the New Testament, Christians are addressed as the "called of God," and this word "called," simply means those who have each had a personal meeting with God in which they've heard his challenge and received his mercy. When Jesus dealt with men and women, he always preferred to do so in a face-to-face meeting. Jesus would do nothing for any man or woman who did not tell him all the truth. Think of how, when the woman at the well of Samaria sought blessing from Him, he first of all, before she received the blessing, forced her to be frank with him by Himself revealing openly all the shameful side of her life. (Wallace, pages 170–171)

The living Christ deals with you and me in the same way. Christ seeks to reckon with us—and that reckoning always includes a complete settling of our account with him as it relates to sin and guilt.

There will always be a day of reckoning. Remember the parable of the rich fool—the farmer who tore down his barns to build greater barns in order that he might store the bountiful harvest with which he had been blessed. He said to himself, "Soul, take your ease—eat, drink and be merry." But he failed to reckon with the fact that there would be a day of reckoning for him. "Thou fool," God said to him, "this night your soul will be required of you." There will always be a day of reckoning.

The inevitable day of reckoning is not just an individual matter. It's a law of life. One illustration from our local Memphis scene will make the point. (And Memphis does not stand alone. Other cities across the country are facing just such a day of reckoning.)

Newspaper and television have called our attention to the desperate plight of the public school system in our inner city: inadequate teaching and educational resources; insufficient educational equipment; buildings that are crumbling, that are hazardous for the children who occupy them. A fact that many citizens of Memphis have overlooked to our personal detriment and to the undermining of a healthy community is this: Although a great many of our middle-class children are in private schools, we will not be delivered from sharing in the price that is exacted by an inadequate public school system. We may say we have no responsibility, that we are paying taxes for public schools as well as tuition for private schools, but we are paying the prices of an inadequate public school system every day.

The day of reckoning comes in the form of crime and unemployment and a vicious welfare cycle that will never be broken, apart from education and job training. The day of reckoning comes in the loss of potential skills, potential concerned and supporting citizens, and even potential leaders in every field of endeavor. The day of reckoning is recorded almost daily in the newspaper.

Shelby County Mayor Bill Morris has had a "think tank" task force working on what they have called "the culture of poverty"—an apt description of our situation. They say that this cycle is "the cancer in our midst." The "think tank" has produced a very significant report entitled, "Free Our Children: Breaking the Cycle of Poverty."

Until we break that welfare cycle and attack head-on the "culture of poverty" throughout our country and address the issue of adequate education and job training, we will continue to live in the midst of blighted lives and blighted communities. When will we become angry enough to start dealing with the causes of rural and urban blight and free little children from the destructive power of what has been labeled "the culture of poverty"?

There is and there will continue to be a day of reckoning in our community and national life.

A second rush suggested by this parable has a more individual focus. It is really a call to *daily debt settling*. The servant in the parable was probably an important official entrusted with considerable financial responsibility; yet he took no initiative in making an accounting to the king. When the time of reckoning came, he was hopelessly in debt. Sin poisons our relationship with God. If unattended to, that poison will become so pervasive that our relationship with God will be completely severed. The prophet Isaiah said, "Your iniquities have made a separation between you and your God, and your sins have hid his face from you so that he does not hear" (Isaiah 59:2).

The discipline of confession and repentance must be a daily part of our lives. One of my spiritual heroes is Brother Lawrence. He lived in seventeenth-century France and found his growth in Christian maturity as a dishwasher in a monastery through what he calls "the practice of the presence of God." Listen to him:

> I think it proper to inform you after what manner I consider myself before God . . .
>
> I consider myself as the most wretched of men, full of sores and corruption, and who has committed all sorts of crimes against his King . . . Touched with a sensible regret, I confess to him all my wickedness . . . I ask his forgiveness, I abandon myself in his hands that he may do what he pleases with me. The King, full of mercy and goodness, very far from chastising me, embraces me with love, makes me eat at his table, serves me with his own hands, gives me the keys of his treasures . . . in a thousand and a thousand ways. (*The Practice of the Presence of God* (Fleming H. Revell, 1985); pages 24–26)

There will always be a day of reckoning, and every day should be a day of debt-settling.

God's Forgiveness Is Greater Than Our Sin

That leads to our next truth—God's merciful forgiveness is greater than our sin.

Isn't Brother Lawrence's a beautiful confession? "I abandon myself in his hands that he may do what he pleases with me. The king, full of mercy and goodness, very far from chastising me, embraces me with love, makes me eat at his table, serves me with his own hands, gives me the keys of his treasures; . . . in a thousand and a thousand ways (he blesses me)."

115

And Brother Lawrence is right! Look at the magnitude of the servant's debt in our parable. He owed ten thousand talents. Now that was a larger sum of money than anybody in ancient Palestine could ever envision. Really, sort of like our national debt! The total annual taxes of Judea, Idumea, Samaria, Galilee, and Berea, according to George Buttrick, amounted to only eight hundred talents, not ten thousand. Second Chronicles 25:6 tells that Amaziah hired a hundred thousand "mighty men of valor" to wage war for a hundred talents of silver. Exodus 38:24 says that all the gold used in the Ark of the Covenant was worth less than thirty talents.

So when we read of a ten-thousand-talent debt, we're not talking about something that could be paid off with a home-improvement loan. We're talking about megabucks!

It was a part of Jesus' style of teaching to exaggerate. We call it *hyperbole*. For his purposes he used exaggeration, hyperbole, to make his point. Ten thousand was the highest number used in reckoning and the talent was the largest currency unit of the time. Therefore, ten thousand talents represented a debt that, humanly speaking, was impossible ever to repay. In a dramatic way, Jesus is telling us that we owe God a debt that we can never repay, But God's love is like the mercy of a king who would forgive a debt of ten thousand talents.

You know what that means? It means that God's love is abundant enough to cover every moral debt that any mortal owes. You need never worry about your shortcomings, your sins, in terms of the *adequacy of God's grace to forgive them*. God's forgiveness is greater than your sin.

How much of the heartache and devastating guilt that cripples and debilitates people would be done away with if people would believe that God's love is deep enough and wide enough to forgive and to forgive to the utmost.

Did you hear about the classified ad that read something like this: "LOST—ONE DOG. Brown hair with several mange spots. Right leg broken due to auto accident. Rear left hip hurt. Right eye missing. Left ear bitten off in a dog fight. Answers to name 'Lucky.' Reward to finder."

Lucky? Of course! That was a lucky dog. He was lucky because with all those things wrong with him, somebody still wanted him and was willing to pay to get him back. Isn't that the story of the gospel? With all of our sin and rebellion, God still loved us enough to pay the ultimate price to win us back to himself. God's merciful forgiveness is greater than our sin.

Don't forget it! God's merciful forgiveness is greater than our sin.

Our Forgiveness of Others

Now the final truth, which is the primary lesson of the parable. *God's for-giveness of us is dependent upon our forgiveness of others.* Now that's a touchy truth, not easy to keep clear. So let's pay close attention to the parable.

The servant who owed ten thousand talents had fallen on his knees before the king and begged, "Lord, have patience with me, and I will pay you every-thing." Of course, there was no possible way he could repay such a debt, but the king took pity on him and forgave his debt. But no sooner had this man been forgiven his debt, than he went out and found a fellow servant who was indebted to him. However, instead of owing ten thousand talents, the man owed only a hundred denarii, about twenty cents. Once again, Jesus exagger-ated to make a point. This was a debt that could have been repaid easily to a patient creditor.

Now get the picture! The man who had just gotten a reprieve from absolute poverty and life imprisonment seized his fellow servant by the throat and said, "Give me the twenty cents you owe me." And his fellow ser-vant begged, "Have patience with me, and I will pay you." Surely those words had a familiar ring! But when the money was not repaid immediately, the man had his fellow servant thrown in prison. No wonder the other ser-vants were greatly distressed and reported what had happened to their lord! We have here a picture of a man without gratitude for his lord's forgiveness and without compassion for his fellow human beings, one suffering from what the Bible describes as hardness of heart.

When the king learned that the very one who had been forgiven a debt of ten thousand talents refused to forgive a debt of a hundred denarii, the king had the servant throw in prison "till he should pay all his debt." Jesus conclud-ed the parable with the words, *"So, also, my Heavenly Father will do to every-one of you if you do not forgive your brother from your heart"* (verse 35).

Stay with me now. The Bible does not teach about a God who refuses to forgive or revokes pardon—or who offers *conditional* love. The prophet Micah made this clear in the Old Testament. He asked the question, "Who is a God like thee?" and then he answered it: not "Who is a God like thee that rides on the wings of the wind and treads on the high places of the earth?"; not "Who is a God like unto thee that confounds the devices of the sinner and holds the wicked in derision?"

But this, Micah 7:18-19:

> Who is a God like thee, pardoning iniquity
> and passing over transgression
> for the remnant of his inheritance?
> He does not retain his anger for ever
> because he delights in steadfast love.
> He will again have compassion upon us,
> he will tread our iniquities under foot.
> He will cast all our sins
> into the depths of the sea.

That's who God is, said Micah—but Micah's word was not enough. The word had to become flesh. So there came Jesus, who "into earth's brackish waters of enmity and hate, poured a crimson flood to make them sweet. Never was any man more unjustly smitten. The world He loved drove nails into His hands and feet. Yet He prayed, 'Father, forgive them'" (*The Parables of Jesus*, by George A. Buttrick (Baker, 1973); page 102).

So, God's merciful love is not *conditional*, not capricious. Then, how does the truth of the parable stand? It stands clear and strong. Only as you forgive others can God's forgiveness of you become real. That's the way it is—only as you forgive others—"No life is open to God which bitterly nurses its resentments. Such a life revokes its own pardon" (Buttrick, page 102).

So God *forgives*, but our capacity to receive and retain that forgiveness as a redemptive power in our lives is dependent upon our forgiving others. Jesus taught that truth when he gave his disciples the prayer we call the Lord's prayer: "For if you forgive men their trespasses, your heavenly Father also will forgive you; but if you do not forgive men their trespasses, neither will your Father forgive your trespasses" (Matthew 6:14-15).

So, what do we do when we have been forgiven? We forgive others fully and freely, without holding grudges or remembering wrongs done to us.

To review the truths of this parable:

One: *There will always be a day of reckoning.*

Two: *The discipline of confession and repentance must be a daily part of our lives.*

Three: *God's merciful forgiveness is greater than our sin.*

Four: *Our receiving forgiveness is dependent upon our forgiving others.*
Let me tie it all together with a story.

Many years ago there was a movie entitled, *Stars in My Crown*. It told of an elderly black man who owned a little farm outside a southern town. Some very precious metal was discovered in that area and suddenly there was pressure on him from many people to sell his land. But he would not sell. He wanted to stay exactly where he was. However, the people in the area would not take "no" for an answer. They did everything they could to make him move. They burned down his barn, shot through his house one night, and eventually threatened to hang him by sundown the next day if he did not agree to sell.

The local Methodist minister heard about the trouble and went to visit the old man. At sundown of the next day, all the leading citizens of the community came to the farm dressed in their white hoods. They were ready to hang the black gentleman if he refused to sell. The farmer came out on the porch to meet them wearing his best clothes. He said that he was ready to die and that he had asked the minister to draw up for him his Last Will and Testament, which he wanted to have read at that time.

The minister read the will and those present realized quickly the old man was giving everything to them. He willed the farm to the banker who seemed so hellbent on having it. He gave his rifle to another of the men there who had first learned to hunt with it. He gave his fishing pole to another. In fact, that old man gave everything he had to the people who were prepared to kill him. *He killed them first with love and affection.*

The impact was incredible. Seeing goodness given in the face of such animosity was more than any of them could tolerate. One by one, in shame, they turned away, and the entire lynching mob disappeared. The minister's grandson had watched everything from a distance, and as everyone departed, he ran up to his grandfather and asked, "What kind of will was that, Granddaddy?"

The old minister answered, "That, my son, was the will of God" (Sermon: "The Sign of Jonah—The Sign of the Cross," Eric S. Ritz, April 17, 1987).

Doesn't that make you think about the *cross*? And thinking about the cross makes us think about God and God's forgiving, self-giving love. This is the way we sing about it:

And when I think, that God his Son not sparing
Sent him to die, I scarce can take it in,
That on the Cross, my burden gladly bearing
He bled and died, to take away my sin.
("How Great Thou Art" © 1953, Stuart K. Hine, renewed 1981 by
Manna Music, Inc. All rights reserved. Used by permission.)

And what does that tell us to do when we have been forgiven?
"Go thou and do likewise!"

Experiencing the parable at a deeper level:

1. Using whatever method you choose (writing, speaking, round-robin in a group setting, music, artwork, acting, other), express this parable as a modern parable. Use contemporary people, settings, and events that correspond to the first-century examples Jesus used.
2. Express the parable using events from your own life that correspond to the events in the parable. What would Jesus say to you?

11. WHAT TO DO WITH YOUR ASSETS

The Talents

Read Matthew 25:14-30

Did you grow up enjoying school talent shows? I can remember some serious, carefully rehearsed shows and a lot more that were slapstick and impromptu, but I don't remember giving much thought to the meaning of the word *talent*. We all knew that talent was being able to sing or play a musical instrument, dance, tell a joke, recite a poem, or do magic tricks well enough to get a round of applause from the class on rainy days when we couldn't go outdoors for recess. If you were really talented, you could perform for a school assembly or even for the P.T.A.

As adults most of us have broadened our definition of talent, but have we stopped to think about how we got the words *talent* and *talented* in the first place? The American Heritage dictionary I use credits Jesus' parable of the talents as the source for our word that means "aptitudes" or "abilities." French and German have the same word. In Spanish and Italian the spelling is *talento*, and other modern European languages have similar words that we could easily recognize as *talent*. The *talents* Jesus was talking about in this parable were money, the largest unit of currency in use at the time. But as word usage evolved, we have come to relate the word to the abilities the master in the parable expected his servants to exercise as they used the five talents, the two talents, or the one talent he gave them.

A Man Entrusted to His Servants. . .

A rich man who was going on a long journey called his servants to him and entrusted them with large sums of money. To one he gave five talents, to another two talents, and to yet another one talent. A talent represented more than fifteen years' wages for a laborer in Jesus' day, so even the man with one talent had a great deal to work with. Scripture says that the master gave "to each according to his ability." No direction was given for the use of the money, but the servants knew their master. They knew "that he was a hard man, reaping where he did not sow, and gathering where he did not winnow."

Therefore, to be faithful to their master's expectations, the servant who was given five talents visited the marketplaces and the money changers, the countryside and the city docks, looking for opportunities to buy and sell and realize a profit. He took risks in the futures markets of his day, and undoubtedly sometimes he lost, but over the long haul he doubled his money. The man who was given two talents found some solid investments in wool and mutton, wine, and oil. Investing in the blue chip stocks of his day, he also doubled his money. However, the servant who was given the one talent trembled at the thought of facing his master and reporting that he had lost the talent entrusted to him. He couldn't think of any investment that would be truly safe, so he dug in the ground and hid his master's money. That was the customary thing to do with savings at the time, especially among the poor.

When the master returned after a long time, he called his servants to make an accounting of their stewardship of the money he had entrusted to them. Both servants who had increased their talents received the same wholehearted praise, "Well done, good and faithful servant; you have been faithful over a little, I will set you over much; enter into the joy of your master." But to the servant who returned just the one talent he had received in the first place, and said to his master, "Here you have what is yours," the master replied:

> You wicked and slothful servant! You knew that I reap where I have not sowed, and gather where I have not winnowed? Then you ought to have invested my money with the bankers, and at my coming I would have received what was my own with interest. So take the talent from him, and give it to him who has ten talents. For to everyone who has will more be given, and he will have abundance; but from him who has not, even

what he has will be taken away. And cast the worthless servant into the outer darkness. (verses 26-30)

Before we look at the primary truths of this parable, let's make note of two points. First, Matthew 25 includes three parables Jesus told about the kingdom of heaven and about judgment. The third parable, Matthew 25:31-46, is often referred to as the parable of the last judgment. ("As you did it to one of the least of these my brethren, you did it to me.") The first parable, the parable of the wise and foolish virgins (which we dealt with in Chapter 1), and this parable of the talents both stem from the same introductory phrase, "Then the kingdom of heaven shall be compared to. . . ." The parables describe what is expected of citizens of God's kingdom.

Second, we miss the point of the parable if we try to make the master who went on a long journey identical with God. In this parable Jesus is telling what is expected of us, not painting a full portrait of what God is like.

We Are Accountable to God

The first truth of this parable is the unshakable fact that we are accountable to God. *All that we have and all that we are is a gift from God, and God holds us accountable for how we use those gifts.* Those who have much in the way of talent and wealth and those who have little are all held equally accountable.

At first glance, this parable may seem grossly unfair. In fact, in a similar parable in Luke 19:11-27, when the one pound was taken away from the servant who had not increased his money and given to the servant who already had ten pounds, the bystanders protested, "Lord, he has ten pounds!"

But let's take a closer look. Note first that the master distributed the talents to his servants according to their abilities. Jesus knew that human beings come with a wide variety of gifts and abilities, with widely different opportunities, advantages, and handicaps. Yet Jesus never let such differences stand in the way of his complete love and acceptance of every person who would receive him. Remember what Jesus said about a certain poor widow who dropped two copper coins worth a penny into the treasury:

Truly, I say to you, this poor widow has put in more than all those who are contributing to the treasury. For they all contributed out of their abundance; but she out of her poverty has put in everything she had, her whole living. (Mark 12:43-44)

Jesus knows us in all our diversity and accepts us as we really are.

Now consider what the master said to the servant who had added two talents to the two he had been given and to the servant who had added five talents to his original five. His response to both was identical: "Well done, good and faithful servant; you have been faithful over a little, I will set you over much; enter into the joy of your master" (verses 21, 23). The amount they started with and the amount they produced made no difference. What the master was looking for was faithfulness in the use of what in reality was his own. These two servants knew their master and carried out his intentions to the best of their resources and their abilities. That is all that was required of either of them. The master's equal acceptance of the two reflects Jesus' words from another parable, "Every one to whom much is given, of him will much be required" (Luke 12:48).

What do we do with our assets? When we have been richly blessed with talents, with possessions, with influence and power in the affairs of the world, we always remember that these assets have been entrusted to us by God. *We seek to know the mind of our Master, and we use our assets in faithful obedience to his intentions.*

But let's look now at the person who is really the central figure of this parable, the servant with one talent. Jesus was warning his listeners—and us—to avoid being like that servant. "He who had received the one talent went and dug in the ground and hid his master's money" (verse 18). Without giving the matter much thought, he did what, in popular wisdom, was the conventional, safe thing to do with money. He had made an accurate assessment of his master's character and way of operating in the world, but he didn't see himself as being able to do more than preserve what he had been given, avoiding loss at all cost.

Did he resent the fact that he was given only one talent? Or did the fact that he received just one confirm his lack of self-confidence? Was he aware of what the other two servants were doing with their talents? If so, he let his fear of failure and his lack of self-esteem degenerate into laziness and inertia. When his master called on him to account for his stewardship, he tried to shift his responsibility for his own inaction by criticism of his master's character and expectations.

Jesus talked to a great many people like this servant with one talent. In its early centuries, Christianity was largely a faith of the disenfranchised—the poor, slaves, women, those from insignificant provinces of the Roman Empire—who were widely regarded as one-talent or no-talent people. But somewhere along the way the disenfranchised have been overlooked in much of the church's preaching and teaching. Maybe we still have some baggage from the time when clergy ranked with the nobility, and the leaders and rulers of society were considered the most important communicants in a parish. And more recently we have reflected the viewpoint of men who shape the world—insofar as anyone shapes it—not recognizing the fact that those with less power respond to life in a very different way. Therefore, we are accustomed to preaching about the sin of pride and about sins that stem from aggressiveness and self-assertion, but we have less to say about the kind of sin Jesus is talking about in this parable. Here Jesus is pointing to the sin of self-depreciation, the sin of failing to recognize the value of what has been given us or to take responsibility for developing it and using it, the sin of refusing to take risks for God's kingdom. And he calls that sin unfaithfulness.

What do we do when we judge our assets to be meager? First, we take a second look at ourselves from God's point of view. We don't accept the valuation of family, friends, or the world in general if they think we have little to offer. We believe Jesus' word that the master gave every servant a talent. And we don't give way to envy of others who have more assets than we do. Nor do we let a retiring nature or timidity stop us from developing our talents or from believing that we will discover new abilities as we grow. We develop our talents to the best of our ability, knowing that we have our Master's authority behind us; and we use those talents faithfully in serving God's kingdom.

This parable is telling us that whoever we are, whatever our talents—great or small—we are accountable to God. Faithful servants make the most of what God has given them, and commit their best to God's service.

Everyone Has a Talent God Can Use

Let's make the point crystal clear: Everyone of us has a talent God can use. Whether its the ability to discover a cure for cancer, to make a million dollars, to cook, to make a garden grow, to run a dishwasher, to teach someone to read, to comfort someone in pain or sorrow, to think a problem through and weigh alternatives, to find a solution no one else has thought of, to make people laugh, to manage details in an orderly way, or to motivate and inspire people to work together—God can use that ability.

Poets speak of the opportunities open to each of us:

> There is waiting a work where only your hands can avail;
> And so if you falter, a chord in the music will fail.
> (from "The Day and the Work," by Edwin Markham)

> Use well the moment; what the hour
> Brings for thy use is in thy power;
> And what thou best canst understand
> Is just the thing lies nearest to thy hand.
> (Johann Wolfgang von Goethe)

Jane Merchant, a poet and writer of devotional literature who inspired thousands of people, was an invalid throughout her life. People came to see her to find comfort and strength for dealing with their own problems. Once when she was asked how she managed to accomplish so much from her bed, she said that she tried to remember something her mother had said to her when she was a child. Jane liked to cut out pictures and paste them in scrapbooks, using the flour and water paste her mother made for her. She wished they could afford paste from the store and sometimes complained about the homemade paste. One day when her mother was especially busy, Jane called out to her,

"Mother, I can't use this paste. It has a crust on it."

Immediately, her mother's reply came back, "Jane, just stir what you've got."

Jane said that when she got discouraged, she tried to remember to stir what she had. Then God was able to supply her with the resources she needed for whatever might come. If we will just stir what we've got, all of us will discover that we have talents God can use.

In one of her prayers, Jane Merchant wrote,

> We thank thee, heavenly Father, that thou dost not require of us that our work be the best that can be done, but only that it be the best that we can do. As thou hast given varieties of gifts, grant each of us to value and use honestly the gifts that are our own, without envying or repining because others' gifts seem greater. In Christ's name. Amen. (*Think About These Things* (Abingdon Press, 1956); page 25)

Every Talent Is Needed in God's Kingdom

Not only do we all have talents, but every talent is needed in God's kingdom. We each have the ability to share God's redeeming love with certain individuals in a way that no one else can. Some of us have talents that are distinctive, that can make a unique contribution in the world. Others have talents that are needed to supply the additional hearts, hands, and strength required for a world of peace and justice and love.

Many of you have read the book, *The Hundredth Monkey*, by Ken Keyes, Jr. (Vision Books, 1982). That book reports a phenomenon scientists observed during their thirty-year study of the Japanese monkey, *macaca fuscata*. In 1952, on the island of Koshima, scientists began providing monkeys with sweet potatoes dropped in the sand. The monkeys liked the sweet potatoes, but found the sand that clung to them unpleasant. One young female monkey solved the problem by washing her potatoes in a nearby stream. Between 1952 and 1958 all the young monkeys, and some adult monkeys who watched and imitated the young, learned to wash off the sand before eating the sweet potatoes. Then suddenly, in the autumn of 1958, all the monkeys were washing their sweet potatoes. Even more surprising, the habit of washing sweet potatoes spontaneously jumped over the sea, and colonies of monkeys on other islands and the mainland troop of monkeys at Takasakiyama began washing their sweet potatoes. Scientists conjecture that when a certain critical number (the hundredth monkey of the title of the book) achieves a new awareness, the awareness then becomes common property and reaches almost everyone (from a study reported in *Lifetide*, by Lyall Watson (Bantam Books, 1980); pages 147–148).

The Hundredth Monkey was written in the hope that if a critical number of people say no to nuclear war, the nations of earth will decide that nuclear weapons must never be used. Other changes have come when enough people became convinced that a new idea was right. In most of the world, cannibalism is no longer practiced, girl babies are not killed, the mentally ill are not kept in chains, and vaccination is accepted as a prevention for disease. People were convinced one by one of these new ideas until finally they became accepted as universal practice. In the lives of individuals and in the life of the world, one person can make a difference. *Whether it's to make a unique contribution or to add the weight of one more voice to support what is right—everyone's talents are needed in God's kingdom.*

The servant who was given one talent failed completely to recognize this truth. George Buttrick says of this man with the one talent:

> He is not a bad man. He is not drunken or wasteful. He is not lacking in a sense of responsibility, or he would have squandered his talent. He is something of a judge of character. . . . What was wrong with him? He lacked imagination (the kind of imagination that a man may cultivate) and he failed in courage!
>
> He did not see that his talent was needed. The ruler is depicted by Jesus as caught in overpowering wrath because one talent was not used. Fourteen talents in all had already been proffered, but his anger knew no bounds because one talent had been allowed to rust. The anger of the story is not hollow melodrama; it proclaims the verity that every talent is needed in the divine economy. . . . The failure of the one-talent man leaves as bad a blotch as if the ten-talent man had been treacherous. It is the one vote which will ultimately redeem politics, and the single voice which will ultimately make a world's insistence on peace. . . .
>
> This man lacked imagination to see that every talent is precious. He depreciated his gift. One of the many surprises of the message of Jesus is His constant insistence on the worth of what others call "obscure" service. He spoke of the crucial importance of "a cup of cold water" given in love. . . . He gave warning repeatedly that it is not in human wisdom to know when a deed is "great" or "small"; that

hidden fragrances of the spirit may give a "small" action the smell of a sweet savor to the end of time. (*The Parables of Jesus* (Baker, 1973); pages 247–248)

Therefore, we need never feel that our life is meaningless because we are not needed. Only God can judge the significance of our abilities and our actions, and this parable testifies that every faithful servant is needed. The plea—"No one will miss me. There are so many people in the church with more ability than I have"—is a modern parallel to the response of the servant with one talent.

And the anger of the master in the parable is easier to understand when we realize that every talent is needed in God's kingdom. (Parenthetically, we might ponder how our Master would judge a society that has traditionally discouraged some of its members from discovering and developing the full scope of their talents, content to keep them "in their place," a society that is now immobilized or apathetic in the face of what has been called a "culture of poverty," which is stunting the talents of thousands.) In God's kingdom, the Master has need of every talent and every gift we have to offer.

God Expects Us to Take Risks for the Kingdom

This parable of the talents is shocking to conventional religious sensibility. Here Jesus is praising the servants who took big risks and condemning the man who did the careful, safe thing. Yet we shouldn't be surprised to hear such a parable from one who said, "If any man would come after me, let him deny himself and take up his cross and follow me" (Mark 8:34), one who never hesitated to oppose those in power, one who set his face steadfastly toward Jerusalem when he knew the leaders there wanted him dead, one who trusted to the last God's purpose for his life and went to the cross for our salvation.

Gerald Kennedy says that the man with one talent lacked the courage to take risks. He yielded to the temptation of safety.

Such yielding, says Jesus, is about as far down as we can go. The treatment of the one-talent fellow seems ruthless and extra severe. After all, he only played it safe. But life is less sympathetic with him than with the man who risks and fails. . . .

The safety psychology has invaded a great deal of our modern thinking and believing. How different God appears to us than to the Prophets. The modern interpreters seem to assume that God is always on the side of stability, even if He has to wink at injustice. He is regarded as the Great Stabilizer and the ground of hope for those who dread change. . . .

The creatures made in the image of such a God should be docile, good organization men, and brimming over with the spirit of togetherness. If they have strange longings they should be denied; and if they get the wild impulse to live dangerously, let them lie down until the feeling goes away. (*The Parables* (Harper & Brothers, 1960); page 92)

In many walks of life, playing it safe seems to have more rewards than taking risks. It is certainly easier and more comfortable. However, from the point of view of God's kingdom, nothing could be more dangerous than playing it safe, for what we don't use, we will surely lose. George Buttrick clearly states that truth as he looks further at the man with the one talent:

His worst fault was that he lacked the courage of adventure. This is the crux of the story. He shrank from risk, though he could have known that nothing is gained without risk. The universe is amazingly fruitful for talents. In a few years five can become ten. It multiplies talents as a harvest multiplies seeds. On the other hand, the universe is amazingly *fatal* for talents. If neglected, if unrisked, they vanish. Hiding them in the ground will not save them; they rot! Power used with discretion and adventure is increased power; power left stagnant is seized with paralysis. "Take the talent from him and give it to him that hath ten." It is not a threat, but rather a sober statement of living law. Feed a capacity for music or for sympathy, and it will grow with an ever-deeper root. Neglect it, and it will disappear like a wraith. "Take away the talent from him!" Employ the instinct for prayer and soon the skies will be filled with spiritual hosts. Bury the instinct and soon those selfsame skies will be as inert as slag! The end of the man who will not risk his virtues is torment of conscience, "weeping and gnashing of teeth," and the poor comfort of "outer darkness."(*The Parables of Jesus*, pages 248–249)

So Jesus is calling us to risk, to spend ourselves and our talents for the Kingdom. Our risk may be a vocation that has little security, but vast opportunities for service. It may be trying something we have never attempted before and risking stage fright, anxiety, and the fear of failure. Risk may mean sharing ourselves deeply with others, knowing that love can bring hurt, disappointment, and loss as well as great rewards. It may mean sharing our possessions beyond any tithe that we had in mind. Our risk for the Kingdom will always mean asking, "Lord, what would you have me do?" and praying, "Not my will, but Thine, be done."

And what of our rewards? Our Master's "Well done, good and faithful servant; enter into the joy of your Lord." That joy is the present companionship of the risen Christ and of those who love and serve him, and it is the certainty Paul expressed when he said, "I consider that the sufferings of this present time are not worth comparing with the glory that is to be revealed to us" (Romans 8:18).

For further reflection:

The early church saw this parable as instruction for how they should live until Jesus' return—which they expected in their lifetime. The fact that Jesus' return was delayed beyond their expectation made this teaching about faithful use of gifts especially important for them, as it is for us.

Experiencing the parable at a deeper level:

1. Using whatever method you choose (writing, speaking, round-robin in a group setting, music, artwork, acting, other), express this parable as a modern parable. Use contemporary people, settings, and events that correspond to the first-century examples Jesus used.
2. Express the parable using events from your own life that correspond to the events in the parable. What would Jesus say to you?

12. LOST AND FOUND

The Prodigal Son

Read Luke 15:1-32

George Murray called the parable of the prodigal son "the most divinely tender and most humanly touching story ever told on our earth" (*Jesus and His Parables*, page 163). George Buttrick says of the parable:

> To judge this parable with our words is futile and sacrilegious—like the attempt to measure the sunrise with the span of our fingers. For it is more than words; it is fashioned from the love which endured Calvary.
>
> No story more instantly touches the nerve of actual life. Let it be read, without comment or explanation, and it conquers us. Its vivid strokes have caught human history. (*The Parables of Jesus* (Baker, 1973); page 189)

Not only has the parable caught human history, it catches our individual histories. In the changing events of our lives it takes on new and deeper meanings from year to year. And at various times most of us have seen ourselves in every major role in the parable: as the son who went into the far country; as that second prodigal, the elder brother; and even as the father. The parable presents so clearly its primary message of the father's forgiving love that many say it should be named "The Parable of the Loving Father." However, each character and each event in this parable is so carefully and so wonderfully drawn that we can find many messages in it, and some of them will be written to our personal address.

This Man Receives Sinners

Jesus told the parable of the prodigal son in response to the criticism of the scribes and Pharisees. Luke records the events in this way:

"Now the tax collectors and sinners were all drawing near to hear him. And the Pharisees and scribes murmured, saying, 'This man receives sinners and eats with them' " (Luke 15:1-2).

To answer these critics, Jesus first told the parables of the lost sheep and the lost coin, showing the supreme effort the shepherd and the housewife were willing to make for one that was lost. In each case, when the lost was found, they called in friends and neighbors, saying, "Rejoice with me." Surely, the scribes and Pharisees should have seen the rebuke in that part of the story. If friends and neighbors were willing to rejoice over a lost sheep and a lost coin, couldn't the religious leaders of a nation rejoice over the fact that sinners were eager to hear a religious teacher? They, themselves, were unwilling to seek the lost souls, but couldn't they rejoice when someone else did?

Far from rejoicing, the scribes and Pharisees considered Jesus tainted by his associations with outcasts and sinners. Therefore, to make crystal clear where God stood in the matter, Jesus concluded each of these parables with the message: "I tell you, there will be more joy in heaven over one sinner who repents than over ninety-nine religious persons who need no repentance" (Luke 15:7, 10).

As an aside, let's not be too quick to congratulate ourselves on being far better than the scribes and Pharisees. Christians—beginning with the disciples—have too often rejected any approach to the faith except their own particular interpretations and practices. One day John came to Jesus and said,

"Teacher, we saw a man casting out demons in your name, and we forbade him because he was not following us."

But Jesus said: "Do not forbid him; for no one who does a mighty work in my name will be able soon after to speak evil of me. For he that is not against us is for us. For truly, I say to you, whoever gives you a cup of water to drink because you bear the name of Christ, will by no means lose his reward" (Mark 9:38-41).

In the 1950's, a tent evangelist came to the northeastern Pennsylvania town where a friend was serving a Methodist church. Among the people who responded to the evangelist's preaching and accepted Christ were a man and woman who had lived together for many years in a shabby little house on the edge of town. They had a house full of children, but had never married. After the evangelist left town, this couple came to my friend and asked him to marry them and to receive them as members of the church. When my friend did so, one of the officials of the church was indignant.

"Do you expect us to associate with trash taken in by a fire-and-brimstone tent preacher? I never thought I would see the day when a Methodist preacher would marry people like that. It's a disgrace."

My friend replied, "The only disgrace is that some preacher didn't do it sooner. In all the years these people have lived in this town, we have never invited them to our church. I'm grateful that a tent evangelist did our job for us."

He Took His Journey Into a Far Country

So Jesus told three parables to his critics. After the parables about a sheep that had strayed and was lost and a coin that had been misplaced—neither willfully wishing to be lost, if we can ascribe such wishes to sheep and to coins—Jesus went on to tell a parable about a son who was determined to lose himself, or who—in the idiom of our day—wanted to tell his family to "get lost."

There was a man who had two sons. One day the younger son came to his father and said, "Father, give me the share of the property that falls to me" (verse 12). According to Deuteronomy 21:17, the oldest son would receive twice the portion of the other sons; in this case, two thirds of the property, while the younger son received one third. When property passed by gift from father to son during the father's lifetime, the legal position was that the son obtained possession of the capital—in this case land and stock—immediately, but the father retained the interest—the unrestricted use of the property—until his death. In this parable the younger son demanded not only possession of the property, but the right to dispose of it. The Greek words translated "gathered all he had" in verse 13 usually carried the connotation, "having sold everything off."

135

Some scholars believe that this younger son's request, which was in violation of custom, would have been a grave blow to his father. In the eyes of the community, and in his own eyes, the father would see this request—which sounds more like a demand—as flaunting the honor and respect due to a father and the loyalty due to the family. Such shocking conduct would evoke pity and gossip, which in our day might be expressed as "he's robbing his own father and trying to push him into his grave."

Nevertheless, the father divided his property between his sons. The older son followed custom and left the use of his share of the property in his father's hands, but the younger son immediately turned everything into cash. "Not many days later," Scripture says, he gathered everything "and took his journey into a far country."

Jesus doesn't tell us much about this young man. Since nothing indicates that he was married, we can conclude that he was probably still in his teens. Most Jewish men at the time were married by the age of eighteen or twenty. We also know that he put what he wanted to do ahead of family ties. That in itself would not have drawn Jesus' criticism. Jesus himself—the oldest son—had left home and had called others with family responsibilities to leave family behind and follow him. When a man said, "Lord, let me first go and bury my father." Jesus replied, "Follow me, and leave the dead to bury their own dead" (Matthew 8:21-22).

But there was a vast difference between Jesus' leaving home and this young man's departure. What Jesus wanted was to obey God's will. He left home with a sense of direction and purpose, and at the time of his baptism he tested that purpose and received God's blessing. Jesus then spent forty days in the wilderness struggling with temptations that centered on the methods he should use in his ministry, and again he received God's confirmation—"angels ministered to him." If the prodigal had a purpose, it was to have a good time. He didn't consult the will of either his earthly father or his heavenly Father before he set out, and he didn't give much thought to the methods he would use in achieving his purpose. He did a very poor job of achieving even the selfish purpose of devoting his life to having a good time.

We can learn an important truth from comparing Jesus' leaving home to begin his ministry with the way the prodigal set out on his journey. The truth has two parts: *First, we need God's guidance and blessing on the direction and purpose of our life journeys, and second, we need to choose ways and means of achieving journey's end that conform to God's will.*

There is a proverb that says, "Even the longest journey begins with the first step." When the prodigal reached the far country, he quickly reaped the results of his first steps—his choice of purpose and the way he went about achieving it. Scripture describes what happened in just twenty-seven words, "He squandered his property in loose living. And when he had spent everything, a great famine arose in that country, and he began to be in want" (verses 13-14).

Our own far countries may not require a physical journey. We can leave the Father's house without ever leaving home. Our journey to the far country begins when we say, "Not Thy will, but mine be done." What we squander may be material wealth, but it will more likely be the abilities and opportunities God gives us to be our own best selves and to give our best for God and others. And when we spend everything that we have—mistakenly thinking it is our own, not God's gift—we can be sure that a great famine will arise in our far country, wherever it is. The famine may be a loss of meaning in life, a marriage that is empty, estrangement from children, a job in which the more we get ahead the more we ask, "Is this all?" Our far country may be addiction to alcohol or drugs or compulsive eating. It may be misuse of sexual relationships.

God Is in the Far Country

Whatever the far country, remember this truth: *God is also in that far country.* How do we know? First, the prodigal realized that he was in want. God's grace awakens us to our need and that awakening is the first step toward our repentance and recovery. Second, the prodigal found a way to survive until he could decide what to do next: "He went and joined himself to one of the citizens of that country, who sent him into the fields to feed swine" (verse 15). No work could have been more loathsome to a Jew, but this young man wanted to live. God gives us the will to live. But still the prodigal's situation was desperate. "He would gladly have fed on the pods that the swine ate; and no one gave him anything" (verse 16). So finally, when the prodigal fully realized where he was and what he had become, "he came to himself"—and that was a supreme act of God's grace.

"But when he came to himself." That is as divine a word as any from the lips of Jesus. Alien from God, we are alien from our veritable selves. It is not a mere manner of speaking which prompts us to say of the irritable or ungenerous mood of a friend, "He is not *himself* to-day." Irritability is unnatural. When the far country has constrained a man in undestined bondage, there is a stirring in his soul—a movement as inexorable as the stars, as splendid as God is splendid—whereby he comes to himself. The man at odds with the austere vision is not the real man. Self-will is not our true self. The far-country can never be our homeland.

Jesus did not make light of sin. He painted its terrible consequences with terrible fidelity. But he could not believe that sin is the act of genuine humanity [as God intended it]. (Buttrick, pages 191–192)

When we come to ourselves, we face the life and death decision, "What shall I do now?" The prodigal remembered his father and his father's house:

How many of my father's hired servants have bread enough and to spare, but I perish here with hunger! I will arise and go to my father, and I will say to him, "Father, I have sinned against heaven and before you; I am no longer worthy to be called your son; treat me as one of your hired servants." (verses 17-19)

So he rose and went to his father. There has been debate about whether this son was truly penitent. Was he still motivated by self-interest, together with the recollection of where he could get three square meals a day? Can any of us be absolutely certain about our motives? Most sins provide some attraction or some satisfaction, or we wouldn't indulge in them. To focus on our sins and to search our souls trying to convince ourselves that we are truly sorry for every moment of sinfulness is not helpful. The important thing is to turn away from sin and to turn toward Jesus. The word *convert* means literally to turn around. The important thing here is that this young man turned around, left the far country, and returned to his father. There comes a time to leave the past behind.

His Father Had Compassion

The father is truly the center of this parable. One commentator sees him as himself a prodigal, an example of moral shallowness: "Had we no deeper insight into the moral problem of sin, guilt, judgment, penitence, forgiveness, and restitution than that provided in this story, we would exculpate prodigals as readily as this man did" (*Parables of Crisis*, by Edwin McNeill Poteat (Harper & Brothers, 1950); page 147). That is just the scandal of Jesus' gospel that the Pharisees couldn't tolerate. Jesus was accepting sinners who had no understanding of the law or of what purity required, who made no attempt to conform to religious requirements, and—instead of first reforming them—Jesus ate with them. He accepted them into table fellowship.

This father exhibited the same shocking behavior. The son had some recognition of his wrongdoing. He had rehearsed his speech of confession, but instead of building on this good work of reform already begun, the father completely ignored it.

The speech of contrition prepared and rehearsed as he had trudged home . . . was never completed. He was not allowed to say, "Make me as one of thy hired servants." For "while he was as yet afar off his father saw him." He had watched for him daily. He recognized him even in his rags. He knew the swing of his steps, the line of his body. Every feature had been treasured in memory, looked at, wept over many times during those weary years. Seeing him at last, the father ran with incoherent joy and kissed the boy again and again. "Bring forth the best robe"—all the marks of the far country must be covered! "A ring on his finger"—token of authority! "Shoes on his feet"—slaves went barefoot, but a son must be shod as befits the family honor! "For this my son was dead and is alive again." There was no word of sharp reproof, no making sure of a sufficient sense of guilt, no requirement of probation, no sentence to quarantine until the disease of sin should have been cured. There was only the fullness of a father's love! . . .

Who is the "*father*" in this story? He is the picture of God, the most winsome picture ever drawn on earth! This parable is the heart of the gospel. God is eager to forgive utterly, and to restore. For there is no forgiveness except utter forgiveness. To "forgive but not forget" is to

139

refuse to forgive. And there is no forgiveness that does not restore.
(Buttrick, pages 193–194)

How consistent this picture of God with Paul's testimony, "But God shows his love for us in that while we were yet sinners Christ died for us." Paul goes on to describe how that love works to lead us into new life. He says, "For if while we were enemies we were reconciled to God by the death of his Son, much more now that we are reconciled, shall we be saved by his life" (Romans 5:8, 10). The saving work begins when we return to the Father's house and are received with open arms.

Martin Luther said that we should be "Christ to our brother." We don't usually think in terms like that, nor do we often think of ourselves in the role of the father in this parable of the prodigal, but sometimes that role is thrust upon us. Sometimes we have an opportunity to offer the open arms and the open door.

Mary Lu Walker, a Roman Catholic laywoman, is known and loved for her songs and for her music leadership in groups of many denominations. She has a loving, close-knit family with eight children, but once one son left home, traveling on his motorcycle, not telling anyone where he was going, and not getting in touch with family or friends for a considerable period of time. Finally, after long, anxious days and weeks, after many prayers, tears, and sleepless nights, a telephone call came, and a question, "Can I come home?" Out of the pain and joy of that experience and the associations she made with the parable of the prodigal son, Mary Lu wrote this beautiful song:

If I ran away today, if I made you cry,
If I traveled far and wide and never told you why,
But if I found the times were hard,
And I was all alone,
Could I still come home to you,
Could I still come home?
Could I knock upon your door,
And would you let me in?
Would you be glad to see me, even though I'd been
So long, So long away from home,
So long, So long away from home.

If you ran away today, if you made me cry,
If you traveled far and wide
And never told me why,
But if you found the times were hard,
And you were all alone,
I'd hope that you'd come home, my child,
I'd hope that you'd come home.
You could knock upon my door;
I'd run to let you in.
I'd be so glad to see you
No matter where you'd been.
So glad, so glad to have you home,
So glad, so glad to have you home.
("Runaway Song," *Dandelions* (Paulist Press, 1975); pages 55–57)

Sometimes we are privileged to share in Christ's work by welcoming the prodigal.

So, the father provides us an illuminating, heartwarming picture of God. When you boil this parable down to its most precious essence, the primary lesson is this: When the prodigal son returned home, the Father received him as though he had never been away.

The Second Prodigal

"So glad, so glad to have you home." That's the way we would like for the parable to end, but it doesn't stop there. Jesus goes on to tell the parable of the elder brother.

Why did Jesus add it? There can be only one answer, because of the actual situation. The parable was addressed to men who were like the elder brother, men who were offended at the gospel. An appeal must be addressed to their conscience. To them Jesus says, "Behold the greatness of God's love for his lost children, and contrast it with your own joyless, loveless, thankless, and self-righteous lives. Cease then from your love-less ways, and be merciful. The spiritually dead are rising to new life, the lost are returning home, rejoice with them". . . . The Parable of the

Prodigal Son is therefore not primarily a proclamation of the Good News to the poor, but a vindication of the Good News in reply to its critics. Jesus' justification lies in the boundless love of God. (*The Parables of Jesus*, by Joachim Jeremias (Charles Scribner's Sons, 1963); page 131)

Let's take a closer look at this second prodigal. When the older brother returned from working in the fields and heard music and dancing, he called to a servant and asked, "What's going on?" The servant replied, "Your brother has come, and your father has killed the fatted calf, because he has received him safe and sound" (verse 27). But the brother was angry and refused to come in and join the party.

Mark now the father's action toward this son. He went out to him, just as he had gone out to meet his younger son, and he entreated him. But the elder son would not listen to his father. He was too full of self-righteousness, self-pity, and a sense of being ill-used. He launched into a tirade,

> "Lo, these many years I have served you, and I never disobeyed your command; yet you never gave me a kid, that I might make merry with my friends. But when this son of yours [not this my brother] came, who has devoured your living with harlots, you killed for him the fatted calf!" [Then his father said to him,] "Son, you are always with me, and all that is mine is yours. It was fitting to make merry and be glad, for this your brother was dead, and is alive; he was lost, and is found." (verses 29-32)

The elder brother had avoided the sins of self-indulgence, but he had given way to jealousy, anger, pride, and harsh judgment. How easy it is to fall into the role of the elder brother! And how devastating. One of the great dangers of the elder brother's sins is that we fail to recognize their soul-destroying power. Society has tended to regard these sins as mere faults, not stigmatizing them in the way it has stigmatized "sins of the flesh." But Jesus took a different view. When we commit these sins we take ourselves as irrevocably outside our Father's house as we do when we go into the far country.

The older son refused to come in. We shut ourselves out. We make our faith a matter of rules and credits, of keeping score. We have not entered "into the joy of our Lord," as the parable of the talents puts it. The elder son did not know the joy of fellowship with his father. He was too busy meeting requirements set up in his own mind. He had never asked his father for a kid that he might celebrate with his friends. He had never asked his father for what his father was waiting and wanting to give him. How sad!

Even more damning, the elder son would not share a roof with his brother. By that act, he was denying himself entrance to his father's house. Jesus was giving the scribes and Pharisees this message: "God has welcomed sinners. If you refuse to sit at the table with them, you are keeping yourselves out of God's house."

The parable breaks off there. Will the elder son accept his father's invitation to come into the house and rejoin the family, rejoicing in his brother's return? The invitation is still open. Jesus came to seek and to save the lost, whether they are in a far country or in their own back yards.

For further reflection:

In many places Jesus explained his mission to the poor and to sinners: see Mark 2:15-17, Matthew 9:9-13, Luke 5:27-32. In other places he pointed out why the outcasts were nearer to the kingdom of God than the scribes and Pharisees: see Matthew 21:28-31 and Luke 7:36-48.

Experiencing the parable at a deeper level:

1. Using whatever method you choose (writing, speaking, round-robin in a group setting, music, artwork, acting, other), express this parable as a modern parable. Use contemporary people, settings, and events that correspond to the first-century examples Jesus used.
2. Express the parable using events from your own life that correspond to the events in the parable. What would Jesus say to you?

LaVergne, TN USA
02 September 2010
195668LV00004B/43/P